STOCK TRADING FOR BEGINNERS:

IDEAS AND STRATEGIES TO START INVESTING FOR A PROFIT WITH A WINNING SYSTEM THAT LEARNS HOW TO MAKE MONEY IN STOCKS AND WHAT YOU NEED TO BECOME AN INTELLIGENT INVESTOR.

Table of Contents

Introduction

With stocks, the rate of return is so much higher than savings, but then so is the risk. As the interest rates of banks fluctuate with the economy, the stock market fluctuates on the principles of supply and demand. Sometimes the stock market performs very well (bull market), and sometimes growth is sluggish (bear market). In adverse situations, like the 2008 stock market crash, stock investments can be wiped out completely. The high returns and accompanying high risk of the stock market compare rather garishly against the low returns and low risk of savings as far as a savings plan for your future goes.

It seems that you are likely to be having the same thoughts or intentions as myself when I first got bitten by the investing and trading bug. I would venture so far as to say this because how else would you be reading this at this very moment if it weren't for the desire for knowledge about the stock market and other financial instruments. Even more so, I would say, would be the want and hunger for specific knowledge on how to make money and create wealth from the same said markets. Am I not right?

I had those exact same thoughts when I was but in high school. It started out as something fluid and intangible, where I just had this tingling bit of excitement at the thought of making some dough just by choosing the right shares and clicking the right buttons. Yes. I am not of the generation where exchanges were dominated by men shouting and yelling. By the time I made my first foray into the stock market, the digital age had already dawned on the financial markets. I am not that old, but daresay old enough to be carving out this collection of what I consider to be rules for anyone, beginner or intermediate or even experts, who want to see more success in the stock market.

I am no famous personality, not a television worthy fund manager nor one of the numerous trading gurus that you can find a dime a dozen these days. You can try googling for me, but chances are you won't be finding much. I term myself as the man on the street investor cum trader. No silver spoon nor special circumstances marked my gradual accumulation of wealth primarily gotten from the stock market. I want you to know this because this means that you can also go out and do what I have done. You can possibly build your retirement fund yourself, give yourself bigger bonuses than what your current boss is giving you, and even become your own boss. I say all these not as words of motivation, but as words of fact. Of course, it will not be that easy. Anything worth having is never that easy, yet what I want to try doing with this book is to make your road just that bit easier.

You can be a complete beginner, just like I was back in high school. Or you can be already well familiar with the Dow Jones and S&P as well as the Russell 2000. This book will act as a guide book for those who are fresh starters and new to the game. It will also serve as timely, constant reminders to those who already have skin in the game.

I made the effort to write this not because of the want for fame or fortune, but because I was primarily thinking of how I wanted to help two of my friends out. One had come to seek advice from me on investing. Being a complete newbie to this, he knew virtually nothing about the financial markets and its myriad of instruments. Another also came to me, but this friend had tried his hand in the markets and gotten burned. Both of them wanted help so I thought this writing would serve to help them out with much better clarity than just conversation alone.

One word of caution however, this is no holy grail. Anyone who sells you the idea that there can be a be all and end all kind of answer to making money to the stock market should be placed high on your alert list. You can still listen on, as I have, but you need to know when you are being taken for a ride, and jump off that bandwagon before you get scammed of money and time.

Think about the Madoff pyramid scheme and countless other human inventions that prey upon the human emotions of greed and fear. Investing money with someone who promises you astronomical returns while having a hard time giving you the exact way of how he goes about doing it is really simply throwing your money down the drain.

Buying this or that automated system and blindly following what the system churns out is also another way of trying to get out of the work that needs to be done. Think about it, when a farmer wants to reap a bountiful harvest, he must definitely plough the fields, sow the seeds and also have the patience to wait. The same goes for you if you wish to become a capable investor in the markets. There will be automated tools which will help us in the journey, but they should just remain as tools, not become the decision maker. You should always hold the final say. That is the reason why practical knowledge is so important in this field. I say practical knowledge because you can definitely read up on all the books surrounding the great legends like Warren Buffett and Peter Lynch, and yet still end up not doing much because you simply do not know how or what to do.

My aim is to allow you the chance to take the wheel in your own hands, and direct your ship in this veritable ocean of financial information. You definitely will not learn all that you need to learn, it would be foolhardy of me to make this claim, but you can be assured that after going through this, you will definitely have the knowledge to make smarter decisions for yourself with regard to gaining wealth in the financial markets. This book does not promise that you can make x amount of money in y number of days like what some other books do. That again would be foolhardy of me to make such a claim, and I do not do foolhardy things.

What I can promise you though, is that the knowledge and information found therein will stand you in good stead whether you are just a beginner, or someone trying to find more success in the stock market. I have shaped the information into what I would like to think of as rules. These are rules which should always define how you approach any investment or trading instrument. At the end of the day, always know this. You are the sole decision maker in the growing of your wealth, and all you should be doing is to gain knowledge and know-how to make that decision making process more robust and smooth. That sounds way different from the easier route of buying a system or relying on another person to make money for you isn't it? It is worth it though, because after all that training and perseverance, you gain something that no one can take away from you.

In the end, a lot of what happens next in your investing and wealth accumulation journey will depend primarily on you. I would like this opportunity to be present during this time in the form of these rules which I have collated from my years of investing and trading so that they might be of some help to you. Read them, peruse them and most importantly, think about them, because sometimes deep reflection may yield unexpected answers.

This book is meant to improve your knowledge of the operations of the stock market, enabling you to understand ways of making good money in investing even while holding on to your main job. I believe that the topics discussed here will arm you with enough information to turn you into a fairly able investor, one that makes distinctly more money in interest on their investment than the bank could possibly give. By following this book's practical and simply written guide on stock market investing, it is our hope that you will become a better investor and convert your current savings into so much more.

Chapter 1 The Dynamics of Stocks

Stocks is just the nickname for "shares of stock" or equities, which represents units of ownership of a certain corporation. So, if you held even just ten shares out of the tens of millions of shares of Intel, Inc., you wouldn't be lying if you said you're one of the owners of Intel, Inc. Seriously, you are! The only issues left for discussion is how much of the company you own, which judging by having on ten shares isn't much. But still, you can have bragging rights.

There's a really good reason why corporations issue shares of stock to the general investing public. And that reason is to raise more capital. The other option is to borrow money, which puts companies under an obligation to pay back the money they borrowed at a specific time and with a specific interest rate. By raising capital through the issuance of shares of stock to the public, corporations aren't saddled with financial obligations and interest expenses. There are some advantages to borrowing money over issuing shares of stock, but for purposes of this book, those aren't relevant. I just wanted you to understand what stocks are from the perspective of both you as the investor and that of the issuing company.

Types of Stocks

There are two general types of stocks issued by corporations: common and preferred stocks. Let's start with the preferred stocks.

Preferred shares of stocks are - as the name implies - a kind of stock that has certain "privileges" over common shares. One is that in most cases, they're entitled to dividends every year. Another advantage is that in case of liquidation of the company, proceeds of the assets will first be distributed to preferred holders before common shareholders. But such privileges have a cost: voting rights.

In most companies, only common shareholders have the right to vote. That being said, common shareholders hold power in terms of appointing the board of directors of a company and voting on crucial matters that might affect the going concern of a company, such as a change in name, change in business, etc.

Listed Vs. Un-Listed

Another way that shares of stocks are classified is being publicly listed. Stocks that are publicly listed can be bought and sold on major stock exchanges such as the NASDAQ in the United States and the New York Stock Exchange (NYSE). Un-listed shares of stocks are those that aren't traded in exchanges and can be very hard to transact in because you will have to personally look for buyers and sellers of a specific share of stock at the right price and your desired volume. So, for purposes of investing or trading in stocks, we will be referring to publicly listed shares of stock, i.e., those that are traded on major exchanges.

The Stock Market

When you hear the word market, what comes to your mind?

A stock market is a place where all buyers and sellers of publicly listed shares of stocks come together to buy and sell such stocks. It's also a place that has all the necessary infrastructure to make huge amounts of trades in a very fast and secure manner from just about anywhere in the world, whether on the actual physical location of the market or anywhere in the world via the Internet.

When we talk about the stock market, we're talking of specific stock exchanges, which are platforms or systems where shares of stocks are allowed to be traded regularly. Examples of stock exchanges include the New York Stock Exchange (NYSE) and the NASDAQ. Through their platforms, buyers and sellers of shares of stocks of many of the world's biggest companies can go to transact easily and securely.

How The Stock Market Works

Corporations that need to raise new capital for expansion to open themselves for investment by the general investing public. This means these corporations open their doors and let thousands or millions of new investors become part owners of the company in exchange for shares of stock of the company. And they do it through what's called as initial public offerings or IPOs, where they sell new shares of their stock to anybody eligible to do so. And once they go public, they list their shares on major stock exchanges like the NYSE and NASDAQ for fast, reliable, and safe facilitation of buying and selling transactions of their shares of stock.

Why are stock exchanges very important? First, they offer convenience in looking for and dealing with counterparties. Let me illustrate.

Let's say you have 12 shares of Apple stock. You bought them at $100 per share, and now you want to sell them at a profit, probably $110 at the minimum. To be able to realize your profit, you'll need to find a buyer for your ten shares of Apple stock. In particular, you'll need to find a buyer who'll be willing to agree with you on two terms: the price you're asking for and the number of shares you're selling. If I ask you right now, do you have any people in mind that you think would want to buy the exact number of Apple shares at the price you want? If you're honest with me, you'd probably answer me with a resounding "no." If that were the case, you still have an option: post an ad - online or offline - hoping that someone would be interested enough to buy your shares. Even then, the odds of that happening exactly the way you want it to would be very low, and if ever you do find such a buyer, it would probably take days or even weeks. That's what happens when there are no stock exchanges.

The other option is, of course, the stock exchange on which Apple's shares are listed. You log on to your online account with a stockbroker through which you can directly access the stock market, which in the case of Apple, Inc. is NASDAQ. Once you're there, you can easily see how much buyers and sellers are willing to buy shares of Apple's stocks on the spot. When you look at the current quotes for Apple's shares (or any other listed share for that matter), you will see two sets of prices: bids and offers (or in some cases, also called "ask"). Bid prices - located on the left side - represent the top 3 prices at which investors are willing to buy Apple's shares and are arranged from the highest bid price to the 3rd highest one, with the number of shares investors are willing to buy. On the right side are the top 3 offers or ask prices, which are the prices that current Apple shareholders are willing to sell their shares on the spot, with the number of shares shareholders are willing to sell. They're arranged from the lowest offer price to the 3rd lowest offer price. The best bid price is the highest price while the best offer price is the lowest offer price and the two are matched directly. If you want to buy shares immediately, you should buy at the best current offer price and if you want to sell immediately, sell at the best or highest current bid price.

Another important reason for trading through an exchange is fast, reliable, and secure payment for and delivery of traded stocks. An exchange's system facilitates the settlement, i.e., delivery of shares bought and remittance of proceeds of shares sold through its member brokers. Brokerage companies often require their clients to deposit a minimum amount of money to ensure payment to your counterparties when you buy. Brokerage companies also require you to have actual shares of stock lodged under your account before you can sell in the market through them to ensure delivery to the counterparties you sell to. Otherwise, they'll be penalized by the exchange, which they'll eventually pass on to you.

Lastly, exchanges are important because it allows both buyers and sellers to get the best possible price on their trades. Because exchanges allow all buyers and sellers to come together under one virtual roof virtually, everybody's aware of how much buyers and sellers are willing to transact. As a result of such transparency, competition becomes pretty stiff among buyers and sellers jostling to get their transactions done as soon as possible, resulting in the lowest possible buying prices and the highest possible selling prices. Without an exchange, it's possible to pay so much for a stock that you can buy at a much lower price or sell shares of stock at an absurdly low price than what you can sell them for because of lack of knowledge of who are willing to transact at the best possible prices.

Trading in stocks involves costs, which you'll need to factor into computing for your desire and actual investment returns. The primary cost involved is the commissions charged by stock brokerage companies through which you'll be able to transact in the exchanges of your choice. Commissions increase your purchase cost and reduce the proceeds from selling your stocks. Therefore, when computing for estimated returns or price targets, don't forget to factor commissions in your computations. $25,000 annually, you'd be short by at least $157,224! But if you invested the money you saved at a substantially higher rate than inflation, then your money can grow enough to more than keep up with the annual increase in the average prices of homes.

The Best Time To Start Investing

Yesterday is the worst time to start investing because it has already gone. Tomorrow is the next worst time to invest because, often, tomorrow never comes, and that leaves us with today!

How To Play High Momentum Stocks

Highly dynamic stocks are those that can grow very quickly in a short time. In most cases, these stocks may also fail unexpectedly and carry significant risks. However, when handled correctly, momentum can be a rewarding method to profit from the stock market.

Definition and risks

Stocks are like humans because they tend to have a relatively consistent specific arrangement. Some actions move slowly and steadily over time, while others move quickly uphill and collapse in difficult times. Stocks that move irregularly are considered very dynamic. Such actions can yield a lot of money, but the losses can also be huge. In most cases, the business prospects of the issuing company are uncertain. Inventories of start-ups experiencing an untested business model or established businesses that are experiencing turbulence tend to be strongly up or down. Because of the inherent risks, you should only commit a small portion of your portfolio to these stocks.

Identify opportunities

There are two main ways to benefit from high-dynamic stocks. You can act quickly or identify a failed action that is about to recover. Momentum traders are looking for a large number of stocks and are looking more closely at stocks that have grown rapidly or lost much of their value in recent years, perhaps last week. When you choose stocks that have made rapid progress and can continue to do so because they have attracted many new interests, compare your recent results with historical trends. If this stock tends to decline after a 40% to 50% increase, for example and has reached nearly 40% in recent weeks, it may be too late to embark. When you're trying to catch up, move away from companies facing insurmountable problems such as debt crises, legal problems, or major scandals.

Reduce your losses

If a momentary trade opposes you, leave. When trading high dynamics, it is especially important to close a losing position to limit the damage. Almost without exception, actions that can generate impressive jumps can fail at the same speed. The most effective way to reduce your losses is to use a stop loss. Before you buy an action, decide how much you will end the agony if the stock price falls and sets a mental limit on the date you want to sell the stock or place an order in your broker's database for automatic execution. Usually, a loss of about 20% is the maximum you should tolerate in any specific trading.

Know the Issuer

Although traders focus primarily on recent share price movements, it is essential to know what is causing them. Once you have identified an action as a potential impulse, study the business and understand the origin of upward or downward fluctuations before committing capital. Make sure the recent earnings are not due to an unfounded rumor or that a major ongoing problem did not cause the accident. After buying shares, keep a close eye on the headlines and feel free to sell if the news suggests an imminent change in the trend.

Chapter 2 Penny Stocks

Have you ever heard of penny stocks? They have been given a bad name; however, they provide you with the opportunity to make a lot of money. There are of course some cases when the bad reputation of penny stocks is deserved however, I want to show you how you can avoid the pitfalls of penny stocks so that you can invest in companies that will reward you significantly for your investment.

Penny stocks are shares that are usually sold for less than 5 dollars. These stocks are not listed on any of the national stock exchange lists. They can be extremely profitable and are very easy for investors to acquire. However, investors have to be very careful that they do not get involved in penny stock scams.

Pros Of Penny Stocks

Because penny stocks are priced so low, they are very appealing for those that do not have or do not want to invest a huge amount of money into the stock market. If one share sells for just 3 dollars you could purchase 100 shares for only 300 dollars. Imagine how much it would cost for you to purchase 100 shares of a larger company like Amazon. I can tell you that it would cost a lot more money. Of course, penny stocks are much easier for a person to acquire. Penny stocks are recommended for those that are just starting out in investing.

One thing that a lot of investors love about penny stocks is that if they do lose money, what they lose is not a huge amount. If you take the example above, even if the market dips, the only thing that you have invested is 300 dollars.

One of the key advantages is that many people have invested in penny stocks only to see their money grow dramatically in weeks or even in a few days. People have watched the price of the stock go through the roof in a short period of time which has allowed them to get a huge return on their investment.

If you are a first-time investor, the price of many of the larger stocks may be a little overwhelming for you. It can take a lot of money to invest in more well-known companies. If you are someone who wants to start investing, who is learning about the market, and is starting out with a small amount of money to invest, penny stocks may be perfect for you.

When you invest in penny stocks, you will be investing in smaller companies. Of course, getting in on stocks when a company is just starting out comes with its advantages. As the company grows your stocks are going to be worth more and more. Investing in penny stocks is a great way to maximize the return on your investment. You never know which of the penny stocks of today will turn into the next Microsoft, Apple, or Amazon!

Cons Of Penny Stocks

Of course, there are some cons to purchasing penny stocks. Nothing in the market is guaranteed and that includes penny stocks.

When you purchase penny stocks you are purchasing stocks in a small company which means that there is no price stability that comes with purchasing shares in much larger companies. Some companies have been found to make false statements in order to boost the prices of their penny stocks. This is why it is so important that you investigate the company before investing in them. The more that you know about the company the less likely you are to get scammed.

Because these companies are not listed on any of the major stock exchanges there have been a lot of fraudulent practices when penny stocks are being traded. You have to remember that these stocks are not governed by a regulatory body which means that they do not have to make specific information public, like companies in the major stock exchanges have to. There are also no guidelines that they have to follow when reporting their finances. This means that you are taking the risk of losing your entire investment if you do not take the time to learn about the company. It can be very hard for a person to tell a fraudulent penny stock from a genuine one. We'll talk more about this in a minute. Lack of information is another con. When you think about purchasing a share in a traditional company you know that you have all of the information about the company at your fingertips. However, when you are thinking about purchasing penny stocks, you may not know if the information about the company is real or if it is fake. Most people would start doing research into the company in order to determine if the information was true or not, however, since the company is so new there may not be enough information out there to determine if the information you have about the stock is real or not.

There are also pump and dump schemes out there. The way that this works is that a person will purchase a huge number of penny stocks. Then in order to make their money back or to make a profit they will send out false information inflating the stock prices trying to sell them to investors. People who are using pump and dump schemes will usually contact an investor via a chat room, a newsletter, through their email, or through a press release. Once the manipulator has sold all of their stock to investors, they have made a ton of money and soon the investors find that they have lost their entire investment.

As an investor you have to know when to sell your penny stocks. However, you have to also be aware that it is really difficult for a person to sell penny stocks. It can be hard for you to find a buyer.

If you are planning on purchasing penny stocks and holding on to them for a long time, they could be a good investment. Imagine how much one you would have right now if you had invested in Netflix when the stocks were penny stocks.

These are just some of the pros and cons that come with investing in penny stocks. Penny stocks may not be very popular when it comes to mainstream investors but if you are able to avoid the schemes and get your hands-on penny stocks for a potentially great company, you may end up getting a huge return on your investment.

Spotting A Pump And Dump

If you are going to invest in penny stocks it is important for you to be able to recognize a pump and dump in case one comes your way. You do not want to end up investing your hard-earned money into something that is going to end up causing you to lose.

1. There is a promise of a return. This goes for pretty much everything in life. When someone guarantees that if you invest a certain amount of money you will profit a different amount, they are manipulating you. All over the internet these schemes play out every day.

When someone promises you or even hints at a promise of a high return with very little risk, the red flags should start going up. This is a warning sign that what you are getting involved in is fraud.

You also have to understand that this can be a broker that is trying to get you to purchase the penny stock. Many times, this is why a person would think that the penny stock would provide them with a return. These brokers or firms are not registered. A firm that is not registered is not legally allowed to provide anyone with investment advice nor are they allowed to sell stocks.

2. An increase in trading. Most penny stocks do not get traded often. So if you are looking at a penny stock and notice that there was no trading in the months prior, but suddenly thousands of shares are being traded, especially if it is happening for several days in a row, it is likely that this is a pump and dump.

When you see a big spike in the volume or the price just before you suddenly get this tip about the stock, you should be aware that this is a pump and dump. This is especially noticeable when the chart has been flat for months at a time.

3. You get a random email about a specific penny stock. Often times, an investor will get emails that are promoting different penny stocks. It is never a good idea for you to follow the advice of these emails. This is one of the most common methods used by many different scam artists, including those that are running a pump and dump scheme.

You may also find that you are getting the same tip from a lot of different sources at the same time. This is because these scammers will hire a promoter in order to sell the penny stock and make their profit.

Of course, this is not an all-inclusive list of red flags that you need to watch for when it comes to pump and dump schemes. However, it is important for you to be aware of what can happen if you invest with the wrong person or in the wrong stock.

Penny stocks because of their low prices can be purchased online in large quantities. While it may sound appealing to an investor to purchase a large number of stocks, you have to remember that it is easy to manipulate penny stocks.

Let's think about this for a moment. When it comes to giant stocks such as Microsoft, it would take billions and billions of dollars for these stocks to be manipulated. On the other hand, just a couple of hundred dollars can manipulate penny stocks.

Penny stocks traded on OTC Bulletin Board markets online. While many people believe that it is best to avoid investing in penny stocks, you need to do what you think is best for you financially. If that includes investing in penny stocks, there are some things that you need to do in order to protect yourself.

1. Read the warnings. The SEC has released many warnings about penny stocks for those that are considering investing in them. If you go to the SEC's main website, you can use the tools located there to search for the company that you are considering investing in and determine if there have been any problems in the past.

2. Understand the level of disclosure. Most of the OTC Markets will rate companies in order to allow investors to see how much information the company has provided. The companies that provide the most information are the ones that you will want to consider investing in. Make sure that you do your own research about these companies and don't just go with the information that they have provided.

3. Always look for a financial statement for any company that you are thinking about investing in, especially if you are considering investing in penny stocks. If you find that there is financial information available, you need to make sure that you analyze it very carefully. Research the company online. Find out if any articles have been written by the company and read the stories of others that have invested in the company.

4. There are thousands of stocks listed on the New York Stock Exchange and the NASDQ. If you are not comfortable investing in penny stock, chances are that you can find a different stock on the NASDAQ or NYSE that you can invest in instead.

Becoming An Excellent Investor In Penny Stocks Without Spending a Dime

Before I go into how you can become an excellent penny stock investor without spending a dime, I want to let you know that this technique will work for any type of stock. I suggest that everyone that is considering investing use this technique before they even spend a single penny.

You can use this technique to practice trading all types of stocks including penny stocks in real time without investing any of your money. This is going to help you learn about the market by using imaginary money.

For this example, we are going to focus on penny stocks. The great thing about this technique is that as you learn about penny stocks you are not going to be risking any of your money.

When you are comfortable and understand trading, you will be able to invest your real money. This is going to reduce your risk of losing your investment.

In order to get started you will begin with 1000 imaginary dollars. You are going to want to decide which penny stocks you would like to invest these dollars in. You should think about it as if you are investing your own real money.

In a notebook you will write down what stocks you want to invest your 1000 imaginary dollars in. Write down the price that you pay for them and then you want to also write down when you decide to sell them, including the price per share.

Invest in a couple of different stocks in order to help you get the most experience. Keep track of which stocks profit and which of the investments would have ended in a loss. See if you can figure out what makes some of them profit and why others end up being a loss. When you invest in one that ends up resulting in a loss, you will want to try to figure out what went wrong with your investment.

Continue to practice investing this way, using imaginary money and tracking your investments until you are comfortable with investing. Then you can start making purchases.

You can use this technique for any type of investment. When it comes to investing, practicing with imaginary money is the best way for you to learn. This will help reduce any losses that you would face in the market and help you gain an understanding of how the market works.

Are Penny Stocks A Waste?

How often I have heard people having conversations about penny stocks. I hear one person who does not understand penny stocks talking to another person who thinks they understand penny stocks.

I hear the question, "Why are they penny stocks," being asked and then the answer, "Because the company has no value and does not produce anything of value."

That simply is not what penny stocks are. Many well-known and massive businesses were traded as penny stocks at some point. Some of the shares in these companies are still considered penny stocks because they cost less than 5 dollars a share. Chances are you know some of these companies.

Ford was one of the companies that was once considered a penny stock. They sold for just under 2 dollars per share. Right now, they are still selling for under 10 dollars!

Pier 1 Imports is another company that started out with its shares being sold as penny stock. In fact, each share cost only 10 cents in March of 2009. Investors who believed in this company purchased those shares and in four years they saw the shares go up to 25 dollars. Today each share goes for about 6.50.

Sirius XM shares sold for as low as 3.14 each and today they are selling for 7.16. While they have more than doubled in value, they are still relatively low in cost.

These are just a few examples of the stocks that were once considered penny stocks. As you can see, these are not shares in companies that are unknown or do not produce a quality product. In fact, these are very well-known companies. These are companies that many people would consider investing in long term in order to watch their profits grow.

There are plenty of wonderful penny stocks out there today that you can purchase. As long as you follow the guidelines that you learned in this chapter and do the research that is needed, penny stocks could be a good investment for you.

Chapter 3 How to Get Started With the Stock

Deciding on how to invest in stocks

There are numerous ways on how to invest in stocks. All of these ways have some advantages and disadvantages, but every individual's situation is different. What's good for you may lead to a problematic situation for another. Considering the period and market value, while looking for stocks to invest in, is highly recommended. Sometimes, the market may be going through a smooth and steady path that your emotional aspects may get in the way. You may invest in expensive stocks due to the success of the market. On the other hand, in a poorly performing market during situations like inflation, you may start to sell off your stocks.

So how can you decide where to invest? First off, you need to analyze how much a certain method of investment would be affected by the level of risk and potential loses. If the risk is too high, but the gains from it would be more fruitful, you would know what step to take. Such decision making requires proper research of all the methods, and a proper understanding of how much would be at stake, in different situations.

Methods of investment

We know that all methods would have certain effects, but at the end, the success relies on how much risk you are ready to take, as well as how much knowledge you have in stock marketing. If you're into a more modern and technological way of business, then you should know, online buying of stocks is a thing.

However, it is only recommended if you are well aware of how the stock market operates, and can give useful advice to yourself, as this one doesn't involve any advices to be given, so you're on your own. Also, it is far more risky, as you are charged only a flat fee for each transaction. Also, to mention, it's time-consuming, as you would have to train yourself until you're confident enough to take the next step.

Investment Club

The next method which you can consider is through the investment clubs. You meet a lot of people who may be going through the same situation you are, and people who can give professional and financial advices. Other people's experiences can make you learn a lot too. It is affordable and can help you to understand and differentiate between different market situations. Increased involvement and investing in stocks through this can help you gain a new perspective and a sense of direction.

Full Service Broker

Then we have a full-service broker. Know that this is an expensive method, as the fees paid to your broker I quite high, but the excess information makes up for it.

The broker will help you with the recommendation and advice on how to take the next step, and the precaution measure to be taken while looking for a good financial advisor. This leads to increased business know-how, more knowledge about the stock market, and increased confidence in your decisions.

Investing in the stock markets

If you purchase some clothes and neglect the fact that trying it on would help you decide whether to purchase it or not and come home to only find out that the clothes don't fit, you'll be pretty disappointed unless there is an exchange or return policy at the outlet. If not, you're at a loss. Trust me, investing in a market is nothing close to purchasing clothes. Hence, neglecting can lead to the loss of a fortune. Louder for the people at the back, investing in stock markets is nothing close to your day to day spending. So, you got to go smart about it.

Investing in stocks for the first time has a much greater risk. However, these risks are to be taken, but there is always supposed to be a margin. The potential risk always needs to be managed. How do you ask? Research gets you a long way. You don't want to trust the company blindly. It is important to analyze and study how the company is doing in the market. Their marketing tactics, financial weaknesses, and productivity need to be kept in mind.

If the business doesn't have a good marketing department, it's likely to go crashing down as soon as the competition gets tough. The finance department needs to be checked and observed at every point, as they handle a major part of the business. Any fishy business being done, the greater is the effect on you. Whatever the business is selling, it needs to have a good production plan, method, and a skilled and efficient workforce.

The trends in the market should be considered at all points

Consumer taste and changes in choices should be properly analyzed, and the reasons behind them should be known. If the owners of the business have enough knowledge about this, and the managers are efficient enough to make this happen, it means your potential risk may be lower.

As a beginner, what is important to take into account, is how the country's economy is doing. Inflation would mean that there can be a sudden downfall in the trends and greater risk of bankruptcy. The time of investing should be carefully chosen. However, it is proven that there never is the perfect time to invest in the market. Comparison of different timings is important. This also depends on the type of goods or services being offered. The price elasticity of demand and supply would help you find out how the market will do during inflation.

Moreover, for long term success, the growth of the company needs to be taken into consideration. Over time, how much the company has actually grown, and what is the difference between its earnings when it started fresh, and what is it now? This determines the stability of the company you plan to invest in. Many businesses go through ups and downs, but the major ones are what you should avoid at all cost. The strength of the industry and how well it does in the market will show how much potential the company has for long-term success.

 Coming on to the other important aspects, the debt and the equity ratio needs to be measured beforehand. If the company is in too much debt and isn't making enough profit to pay it off, it would call for liquidation, which means selling off the assets of the company. You won't be left with anything in this case.

Two kinds of Markets, and How to trade them

Several markets facilitate trade in exchange for assets. Each market runs under different trading mechanisms, which seem to affect liquidity and control of the company. Positive effect on the liquidity of the market would mean the ball being in your court.

The Dealers market

The dealers market is the type of market in which the dealer acts as counterparty between the seller and the buyer. He sets the bid and asks the prices for the security in question. Any investor, who accepts the price, would be involved in the trade. The term 'over the counter' dealers emerged from this when securities are sold by dealers. This leads to increased liquidity in the market, which means a lesser risk of bankruptcy and loss. The market would be able to get out of its debt without selling the assets. This would happen at the cost of a small premium. In this, you would be able to expect an additional return, for holding a risky market portfolio, instead of risk-free assets.

In this market, the dealer holds counterparty risk. He often sets the bid prices lower than the market price and asks for higher prices instead. In this way, the spread between the prices will be the profit the dealer would make.

Such markets are more common in bond and currencies, instead of stocks. There are more future opportunities for many dealers in this market. It holds more long term future success and option, as well as useful for derivatives. One important aspect for this is that foreign exchange markets are usually dealt with within the dealers market. The banks and currency exchange acts as the dealer intermediary. The dealer market is known as the most liquid market. Hence, it is good for you, as a beginner, as paying the debts would be easier.

The Exchange market

Moving on, we talk about the exchange market. Out of all the markets, this one is known to be the most automated, but the irony is that, without the presence of a buyer and the seller, there is no execution of the trade.

In this certain market, no brokers are used for stock trading, as the order books match the buyers and the sellers. This is a quicker and less time-consuming method, which also avoids any delay in the trade to take place. However, the buyers and sellers are expected to find their counterparty, as there is no involvement of a broker or a dealer intermediary. Exchanges are most appropriate for standardized securities. These include stocks, bonds, futures, contracts, and options. Exchanges will typically specify characteristics for the securities traded on the exchange.

Chapter 4 Categories of People Who Invest In the Stock Market

Understanding Value Investing

Value investing is an investment philosophy adhered to by many of the world's wealthy. Individuals such as Warren Buffett and Seth Klarman have stated that they adhere strictly to the philosophy.

Value investing involves a system where undervalued stocks are purchased at a cheap rate. Value investors stake their money on a stock's outlook improving over time. Disregarding whether the company is experiencing a loss at the moment or not.

During periods when companies experience distress, causing their stock values to plummet, value investors swoop in to salvage from the wreckage. They invest in the shares of these companies, hoping for a bounce back.

Value investors do not put a lot of premium on how the public react to tragedies in the economic sector. They rather carry out their own personal research, choosing not to rely on how the bulk of the people respond to drastic downturns in the industries. As a result of this, in some instances, they invest in companies the public have written off. And in the long run, make a huge profit as a result.

Furthermore, value investors understand that a lot of investors do not know so much about stock investments. Thus, it is sometimes possible to find a stockholder relinquishing their stocks at low prices.

In this sort of situation, the value investor makes use of that opportunity to grab good shares at lower prices. Also, value investors hold the opinion that the stock market may not ordinarily reveal the real value of a stock. They disagree with the philosophy of the efficient market hypothesis. The efficient market hypothesis holds the claim that stock prices reflect the true standing of a company at any time.

Individuals who are value investors exercise a lot of restraint. This is because they usually have to wait after their purchase for the stock's price to rise. In this way, they minimize their losses, in the event of one occurring. This is because, from the onset, they had purchased the stock at a cheaper rate than it was valued.

Value investing differs in many respects from speculative stocks. This is primarily because the track record of the parent company guarantees that the value of the stock goes up. The case is not the same for speculative costs.

In addition to this, value investors are more likely to go against the herd than not. In the instances where people are purchasing stocks, they'd most likely be selling. And in the event that the reverse is the case, they'd more likely be selling.

Value investing, as a concept, was introduced by the duo of Benjamin Graham and David Dodd. They came up with this concept in the early 1920s while teaching at the Columbia business school. Subsequently, they were able to author a book; 'Security Analysis.'

At the time they developed the idea, the world of investing was mostly speculative. Graham believed that proper research had to be carried out before any investment in stock was to be undertaken. For a long time, Graham taught this topic at the Columbia Business School, beginning from 1928. His students included even Wall Street professionals.

Over the years, the world of investing has undergone a lot of challenges. However, value investing has remained to be one of the best systems for managing finances.

One of the ardent followers of the Graham school of value investing is Warren Buffett. Year after year, Buffett's finances have continued to climb, and he has been named World's wealthiest person severally. Buffett has always maintained that the secret of his success was his investing pattern, mostly, value investing.

In his own type of value investing, Buffett looks at a company as a whole. He also considers how well the company has done, choosing then to purchase the stock to give him a stake in whatever venture that is. Buffett follows the principles laid down in Graham's book, 'Intelligent Investor.'

In that book, Graham had used a character known as Mr. Market to explain how the securities market can be exploited by an investor. The principles laid down in the book formed the foundation of Buffett's investment decisions. As a rule, Buffett only invests in companies he has an understanding of. Severally, he has turned down investment opportunities in enterprises he did not understand its inner workings.

Amongst them are tech startups such as Google. The reason for this, he says, is so he would be able to predict how well the company would perform.

Buffett believes that one is to invest in stocks as though one is purchasing the entirety of the company. Thus, anyone seeking to purchase any stock has to perform a thorough check on the company. Buffett does not pay attention to how society views the company. He focuses on determining the company's capacity to make profits.

Before deciding on whether to purchase a company's stock, Buffett considers some options. First, he checks whether the company has consistently performed well. One of the ways of determining that is by checking if the shareholders are making a profit on their shares. This is known as Return on Investment.

Further, he checks how the company manages her finances. His inquiries would include confirming if the company was in debt. At the end of all of these series of inquiries, Buffett then begins to invest.

Buffett's species of value investing is one unique to him and his personality. It takes into account his personal philosophies regarding how a business is to be run and managed. Over the years, he has consistently shown how invaluable value investing is to the investor. His template, no doubt, is one that would be emulated even centuries after now.

Merits of Value Investing

There are several benefits a value investor gets as a result of engaging in value investing. Some of them include:

Value investing maximizes your experience or lack of one

For an individual to become a value investor, he does not need to have a lot of experience. He does not need to have been investing for a long time. Also, he does not need a truckload of money before he can begin.

For one to become a value investor, he only needs patience and grit. The person would have to realize that to learn to be patient.

Also, the person would have to understand the idea of delayed gratification. This is because the fruits of value investing are not immediate. For the person to begin to make a profit, he needs to wait for a while. This ability to wait for one's reward – known as delayed gratification – is something any potential value investor will learn.

However, these requirements are not strenuous. Following the above criteria, it can be seen that almost anyone can become a value investor. Thus, the process is not hard, meaning that a large group of people can engage in the venture and make a profit in no time.

Value investing has relatively low risk and volatility

Value investing is usually a long term venture. As a result of this, it is usually immune to the fluctuations that happen in the stock market.

A lot of short terms investments are affected by the volatility of the market. This is because investors in that area are always in the process of buying and selling. The immediacy of such projects then makes them vulnerable to market forces.

Also, the value investor does not have to spend time fretting over how well or not the stock is doing. He basically just purchases the stock, leaves it there and continues with his business. This has the benefit of being a more wholesome approach to investing.

A lot of the mistakes by investors are made when the investor tries to beat the time. Determining when the right times it is to sell and whether to sell at a particular time or not can be daunting. Oftentimes, the pressure from all of that can lead the investor into making errors.

All of these are absent in value investing. The value investor takes his time, weighs his pros and cons before cashing out. Due to the singular fact that he takes more time to come to a decision, he usually makes more profit.

Risk VS. Reward Ratio Is Pretty High

Basically, value investing makes you money. The idea is very spectacular because one buys stocks that are undervalued and makes a huge profit from it over the long run. Evidence abounds that the process works. You only have to look at billionaires such as Warren Buffett to admit there is some truth to the school of thought.

Furthermore, what makes value investing quite appealing is the risk versus reward ratio. Comparatively, the rewards from value investing far outweigh whatever risks that exist for the investor. In the first place, the investor purchases the stock below its actual price. Meaning that even if there is an eventual loss, the investor would not be losing so much.

On the other hand, if the stock eventually experiences a turnaround, the investor reaps huge rewards. In all, it looks like an almost win-win situation for the investor.

Demerits of Value Investing

Notwithstanding that it looks like value investing has no demerits, disadvantages actually exist. They may not be as significant as the profits, but they need mentioning nonetheless.

Figuring Out the Intrinsic Worth of a Stock Can Be Difficult

It takes some level of expertise for one to identify undervalued stocks. A lot of factors have to be taken in by the investor to determine this. The information needed by the investor to make such decisions may not be readily available. Also, a lot of investors may not have the skill to make such a decision.

Going further, there is the fact that the intrinsic value of a stock can be indeterminable. In this, I mean that it could vary from one investor to the other. It may be hard determining exactly if a stock is undervalued or not, thereby compounding the investing process further.

Also, there are chances of being wrong about a stock's intrinsic worth. Even after being prudent about taking in all the factors in determining stocks worth, you can still be wrong. The investor may not be able to factor in such indices such as changes in the leader, etc.

The success of value investing lies in the investor is right about the stock's intrinsic worth. In the instance that he is wrong and the stock is valued less than he pegged it, automatic loss ensues.

Value Investing Requires Hard Work

It has been earlier stated that value investing does not require a lot of experience; that is true. One thing that is also true is that the investor usually makes up for his lack of knowledge by his hard work.

From the very beginning, value investing involves diligence in carrying out researches. Also, the investor needs to have a lot of patience for his investments to ripen. Considering these factors, some investors may tend to give up on the way.

Value investing is not for the faint-hearted. It requires a lot of grit, determination, and patience. Well, this wouldn't matter so much except that in the world we live in today, such virtues are in short supply.

The Expected Yields May Not Turn Up

The beauty of value trading lies in the fact that one buys the stocks and waits for them to get valuable. However, there may be instances where the expected yields do not turn up.

Thus, the investor could end up with a company's 'useless' stock for a long time without breaking even. After holding on to the stocks for a long time, the investor would have to let it go. Although such instances may be few, they nonetheless exist.

Every potential value investor needs to take all of these into consideration before investing. The knowledge of these potential pitfalls would eventually help the investor avoid them in the future.

People Who Invest In the Stock Market

Day Traders

Day trading involves the buying and selling of stocks and other securities within a limited period. The day trader usually completes his transactions within the length of a day.

It usually occurs in the Foreign Exchange (FOREX). The day trader aims to make a small profit on each transaction. The profit eventually then gets to the point where it becomes substantial.

Day trading is a very risky enterprise. In fact, a lot of established investors do not engage the practice, claiming that the risk is not worth the turnover. However, there are others quite committed to the venture.

Day trading is supposed to be some sort of passive income. The day trader just makes the transactions at random hours during the day while maintaining a regular job. But to make the most of day trading, the investor needs to begin to see the task as a full-time job.

The bulk of the profit made by the day trader is done relying on the market's volatility. A day trader is usually attracted to stocks that change position throughout the day. A stocks position may fluctuate because of a number of factors such as market sentiments or general bad news.

Also, day traders also wont to go in for stocks that are liquid. This is because it helps them change their positions without altering how much the stock is worth.

It is possible to find a day trader buying and selling the same stock several timed during the same day. In those kinds of situations, they are usually looking for the most favorable outcome.

Features of Day Trading

There has to be an abundance of capital: This is necessary because of the level of risk day trading entails. The day trader only invests capital he can lose. This makes them bolder in their investments, ensuring they can put in whatever amount without feeling any qualms.

A day trader risks their profits in order to make gains. In some peculiar cases, they even put their capital on the line. It is because of these reasons that it is advised that a day trader have access to funds before beginning.

In-depth knowledge of the marketplace: Day trading should not be entered into by a novice. Individuals who lack the requisite knowledge of the entire structure often incur huge losses.

There has to be a strategy: the day trader isn't expected to begin trading without a well thought out plan. One of the strategies employed by the individual could be swing trading or arbitrage. He engages in it for so long until he masters it effectively.

Day trading isn't exactly a walk in the park. A lot of investors fail woefully even from the start. This is usually as a result of either unfair competition from experts or psychological biases.

For the former, Retail day traders are usually novices to the game of investing. Most times, they fail to have the level of knowledge and experience of the other investors. As a result of this, the experienced investors take advantage of their naivety to make a profit at their expense.

Then for the latter, day traders sometimes sell off their winning stocks too early. Of course this can be chalked up to their ignorance. The times they sell too early, they lose the opportunities a turnaround would have given them.

Beginning as a day trader does not require so much from you. Just to be on the safe side, you could consider opening a practice account first. When you try your hand at the investing game, it will reveal whether you are cut out for that sort of stuff or not.

Mid Term Traders

These are also known as medium-term traders. Unlike day traders, medium day traders maintain a certain position for a few days. This is as opposed to the day trader whose transactions must begin and end in one day.

Midterm trading occurs between two to five days at the maximum. In some rare cases, a trader who begins and ends on the same day could be considered a day trader. This happens if the individual's aim was to reach a particular target, not necessarily to spend just a few hours.

Furthermore, mid-term trading does not require as much capital as day trading. Conversely, it also has fewer opportunities than day trading. In this vein also, medium trading doesn't expose the trader to a lot of risks. The investor – or trader - only invests when favorable options are presented to him.

Another benefit medium trading has over day trading is in the presentation of opportunities. Principally, this is due to the fact that medium trading occurs over a relatively long period. In that case, there are more opportunities for multiple entries and exits.

Midterm investors take advantage of technical errors in the system. They are conscious of when the indicators all align. Medium trading involves the application of several trading principles such as support and resistance, math-based indicators, etc.

Mutual Funds

A mutual fund, typically, is a company that invests money for a group of people under a portfolio. No single person in the portfolio owns all of the investments under the portfolio. In addition, unlike the situation with owning stocks, a mutual fund does not give the investors the right to vote.

Simply put, mutual funds pool the resources of a group of individuals together to form some sort of company. This company then buys shares in another company or even government bonds. Because of the nature of this arrangement, the mutual fund investors do not own the shares directly. However, they still share in the profits and losses of the company.

An investment in mutual funds represents an investment in separate funds at the same time. In this scenario, the investor owns different stocks at the same time. The fund is managed by professionals.

Every member of the mutual fund contributes some fee for the running of the fund. This is known as an expense ratio. This is not taken directly but is calculated based on the value of the shares of that particular investor.

Investors in mutual funds make a profit through a number of ways. They include income from the sale of the securities held in the fund. Sale of these securities usually happens when there has been an increase in their value. When such a sale happens, the gains are evenly distributed amongst the investors.

Also, there could be situations where the value of the securities increase but are not sold by the fund managers. In this case, the individual investor can decide to sell his own shares. Though the entirety of the mutual fund may not benefit, that particular investor makes some profit.

Finally, income can be generated through the sharing of dividends from the stocks held in the mutual fund. The investor can be given an option whether to cash out or re-invest his own share of the dividend.

Of course, like in every investment plan, there is the risk of incurring some losses. However, in the case of a mutual fund, the losses are ameliorated because of the diversification in mutual funds. The risks are spread over a number of companies with different securities.

This would be different if the investment was in a single company's share. If this were the case, a loss suffered by the company would portend dire consequences for the investor. This, however, would not be the case with a mutual fund.

Another benefit of a mutual fund is that they are really affordable. The minimum capital requirement for investment can be as low as $100. Even better, some broker may waive the requirement if the investor makes direct deposits to buy shares.

Also, the funds are managed by a professional. The investor need not have prior knowledge of the process before investing.

This is particularly important when the investor is engaged in other activities. Through this process, the investor gets an investment manager at a very cheap rate.

There are different kinds of mutual funds an investor can engage in. One of them is stock. Stocks are the securities with the highest risks for the mutual fund investor. They are also the most popular type of all the mutual funds.

Another kind of mutual fund bonds. They usually do not carry the number of risk stocks has. There are many kinds of funds existing. Any potential investor needs to carry out proper research before venturing into the investment.

Finally, there are balanced funds. This type of mutual fund is made up of a mixture of stocks, bonds and other types of securities.

Hedge Fund

A hedge fund has striking similarities with a mutual fund. Particular attention has to be paid in order to point out the difference.

A hedge fund is an investment pool that is made up of a limited number of partners known as investors. The fund is then managed by an individual whose main duties would be to maximize profit and limit losses. This individual is known as the general manager while the investors are known as limited partners.

The limited partners are the main contributors of funds for the partnership. While, as earlier stated, the general manager manages the fund following the strategies already spelled out.

There exist distinctions between a mutual fund and a hedge fund. The differences can be found in their characteristics. For a hedge fund, there is usually a limit to the parties that can invest. The fund is open to only investors with a particular amount of funds.

When one meets this requirement, he is known as an accredited investor. The rule stipulates that to qualify as an accredited investor, one has to have an annual turnover amounting to $200,000. Government regulations stipulate that outside of the accredited investors, hedge fund managers can only accept 35 others.

Furthermore, a hedge fund has a wider range of investment options. A hedge fund can invest in anything ranging from real estates, currencies and so on. Here also, a hedge fund has a certain private feel to it. Because of this, they usually lack some measure of governmental – or any other kind of control.

The laxity enjoyed by hedge funds affords them the opportunity of taking riskier moves. This can work both for and against the hedge fund.

A lot of great investments have been made by hedge fund investors who enjoyed such latitude. On the other hand, a lot of investors have lost huge sums of money because of this lack of accountability.

Finally, hedge fund charges not just an expense ratio. In addition, a performance fee is also charged. The hedge fund manager engages in a practice known as 'hedging.' This is where the name 'hedge funds' is derived from.

Hedging involves a complex system employed by the manager to maximize profit. The fund manager usually goes long on the stocks in the instance where they expect a rise in the market. Alternatively, they could go short on the stocks when they expect a drop. Fundamentally, the hedge fund anticipates making profits whether the market goes up and down.

Types of Hedge Funds

Macro Hedge Funds: In this sort of arrangement, the investor's aim is to make profits from macro variables. Primarily, the investor invests in securities with the aim that the macro changes would benefit him. Such anticipated macro changes may include a rise or fall of interest rates, etc.

Equity Hedge Fund: This can operate within the peculiarities of a particular country. It can also be global. Here, the hedge fund prioritizes investing in stocks while hedging against shortfalls in the stock market.

Relative-Value Hedge Fund: Here, the hedge fund maximizes price to bring profits.

Chapter 5 Picking Winning Stocks

Finally! The moment you've been waiting for: time to buy your first stock. Now that you have an account set up with the broker you chose, you need to tell them what to do. Sit down with your plan and take a look at the mix of stock types you've decided will make up your portfolio. Now we'll begin to look for stocks to fill them. Here are the things you should look for in each and every company you're considering investing in.

-What To Look For

These factors work together to determine the overall value and promise of a company. All or most of these need to be strong to make buying a share of ownership in the company a good idea. These factors together will give you an overall picture of the health of the company now and a clear window into its likely health in the future.

-Revenue

This is the first line on an income statement. Revenue is how much money a company is bringing in the door, not accounting for expenses or any other adjustment. When looking at revenue, what you're hoping to see is a steady increase over a decent period of time. Within the same year, quarterly reports may fluctuate wildly depending on the type of company, but you want to see a year-to-year incline in revenue overall.

-P/E

This abbreviation stands for Price-Earning Ratio. A lot of experts consider this the single most important number to look at when considering purchasing a stock. While that is debatable, it is certainly very important. The P/E is a single number representing the result of some simple math. First, the company's overall earnings are divided by the number of shares outstanding, giving the Share Earnings. Then, the price of the stock on the market is divided by that number. Here's an example:

Company X earned $500,000 last year and has 10,000 shares outstanding. This means its share earnings are $50. If the stock is selling for $200 per share, the P/E of this stock is 4. Whether you're looking for a low or higher P/E is based on the amount of risk vs reward you're looking to assume with the purchase. If a stock is a good value, its P/E should be low compared to other companies in the same industry.

-Net Earnings

This is the revenue minus all of the expenses the company incurs. It's easy to think that a higher net earnings line always means the company is in a better position than one with a lower net earnings, but this isn't necessarily true.

Some reasons a company might show a low net earnings but still be strong are restructuring, major innovation or product development, and changes in management. These could improve the earnings for the upcoming years greatly. Net earnings is an important factor, but it's just as important to look at it in the context of the other facts about the company, and the industry at large.

-ROE

Return on Equity is the measure of how well the company is using the money that it makes to improve share value. It is calculated by dividing the net income for the full year by the shareholder's equity (the total of all assets minus the total of all liabilities. Note: preferred stock should also be subtracted as a liability. It is not part of common equity.) This number should again be low relative to other companies in the same industry.

-Debt Ratios

This is the ratio of all debt to all assets. You'll usually see it notated as a percentage or decimal. A high percentage doesn't always mean the company isn't being managed well. As with ROE, look at several years averaged together and at other companies within the same industry.

-Future Earnings

Obviously, we don't have a crystal ball, but we can get an idea of how a company will probably do in the near future. Companies publish "forecast future earnings." Be aware, though: these are the opinions from within the company and tend to be overly optimistic. In order to glean a picture closer to reality, look at forecasts from the past and compare them to the actual performance, and that will give you an idea of how far from the mark the reports tend to be.

-Competition

In all of these measures, you've been comparing each value to the same value of other companies in the industry. While you have that in front of you, take a closer look at the competition. If they have new products that look promising and innovative, that could make the stock you're looking at less attractive. Most importantly, looking thoroughly at the competition will give you a clear picture of the landscape in which you are looking to invest.

Where to Find Information

When a company goes public, allowing its shares to be traded on stock exchanges, it has to file reports on its earnings and the state of its financial health in order to stay in good standing with the Security Exchange Commission. This is great news for us because a lot of the information we need to buy with confidence is contained in those forms. There are three commonly published forms, the 10-K, the 10-Q and the 8K. These all contain different information for different periods of time, but looking at all or some of them will give you an insight into the following aspects of the company.

The 10-K is released once a year and contains the fiscal information for that year. It is audited by an outside accounting firm.

A 10-Q contains some of the same information, but covers only a 90 day period of time and isn't usually independently audited

An 8-K is not released on a set schedule, but whenever major changes are going on within the company. Good things like acquisitions or deals the company has made are included, as well as bad news like SEC investigations. Any material event that could affect the shareholders is an inducement for the release of an 8-K, and it isn't unusual for several to be filed throughout the year.

Honestly, these forms do not make for the most exciting reading. They contain a lot of dry facts with no pitch or polish. That's what makes them so valuable for investors, though! The facts are exactly what you need to make a decision.

-Stock Screeners

This is a ton of information to look at for each stock you want to buy, but there's really no way to be a smart investor without doing it. Luckily, software specifically made to filter through the mountain of data available can help. Stock Screeners allow you to set the parameters of stocks you're looking for, such as relative risk, debt ratios, stock type, and a lot of the other determining factors we've discussed. Then, it only shows you the relevant information for stocks that fit those parameters. This can be an invaluable time saver, especially when first building your portfolio.

-Analysts

Television and the internet are full of opinions on investing. While some of these sources are invaluable, a lot of them are better at getting attention than providing useful advice. Finding analysts whose opinions you respect and whose values align with your own may not be easy, but it will be worth it because you'll have something to check your gut instincts against.

Chapter 6 Exchange Traded Funds

Exchange traded funds are my favorite kind of investment. You'll see why in a second. Mutual funds are diversified, and it is easy to invest in mutual funds using dollar cost averaging. But, they cost money, and you have little control, which you've handed over to a money manager. Also, mutual funds only trade once a day after the market closes. Buying stocks gives you more direct control. Rather than having a money manager you have to pay to carry out his services, including making copies at the office, paying for phones and other incidentals you probably don't like paying for, with stocks you're the one doing the trading. This has some risks, but for those who want control over their investing, it has appeal. Also, you may like the flexibility of being able to buy and sell any time the markets are open. However, due to the buying power of a large group of individuals and a money manager who is working on the markets full-time, it's hard to get the kind of diversification and other benefits that you're going to get with mutual funds.

What if you could wave a magic wand and combine the best of mutual funds with the best of stocks? Well, it turns out that you can. The result is the exchange-traded fund. When you boil everything down to basics, and the exchange-traded fund is an unmanaged mutual fund that trades like a stock.

An ETF gives you automatic diversification – its biggest advantage. Even if you don't exclusively trade in ETFs, it's a good idea to have them as a significant portion of your portfolio.

Typically, an exchange-traded fund will track some kind of stock index. There are a wide array of exchange-traded funds; they also track bonds, real estate, cash, commodities, currencies, and baskets of assets. The price of ETFs changes throughout the day as they are traded on the major stock exchanges. So buying or selling an ETF is just like buying or selling a share of Apple or General Motors.

Like with mutual funds, you may see a lot of discussion of asset classes on websites for investment firms that have created ETFs. There are five asset classes:

1. Stocks

2. Bonds

3. Money market instruments (cash)

4. Commodities

5. Real estate

In contrast to mutual funds, in addition to being able to trade them in real time rather than waiting for an end of the day settlement, many ETFs have larger volumes than mutual funds. They also have lower fees, in some cases much lower. As a result, they are a very attractive option.

For the beginning investor, ETFs are highly recommended. It's a way to get in on your own and have some protection by utilizing the built-in diversity that ETFs have. You can buy ETFs using market orders through your own online brokerage if you know the ticker symbols of the funds you want to buy. They are a great way to do individualized dollar cost averaging. You can buy shares at regular intervals as part of your investment strategy.

The low-cost core is the first class of ETFs we will look at. These are divided into:
- U.S. Equities
- International Equities
- Fixed Income

If you click on U.S. equities, you will see that there are several funds that have different options for tracking major parts of the stock market. For example, they have three options available for tracking the S&P 500:
- Growth
- High-Dividend
- Value

If you look under the general category for U.S. equities (not the low-cost core), you will see that you can also simply track the S&P 500 using SPY. Our friends at State Street work like a mutual fund, in the sense that they've used a large sum of money to buy stocks in the 500 companies that make up the S&P 500. You can buy small shares of it. At the time of writing, the stock is priced at about $285 per share.

However, SPYG – the S&P 500 Growth fund – is only $37 a share (prices will vary, by the time you read this). The fund also tracks the S&P 500 index but gives you a low-cost way to get in the market. However, this fund is designed to tap companies in the S&P 500 that are believed to have the most growth potential. According to the website, they base this on the revenue growth, price to earnings ratio, and momentum of the companies chosen for the index.

You can also use SPDR ETFs to invest in preferred stock or commodities. GLD allows you to buy gold shares. NANR is a natural resources fund that you can use to invest in energy, metals, mining, and agriculture. You can also invest in bonds, loans, U.S. government treasuries, and overseas investing like China or Japan.

SPDR is not the only company out there. A recent arrival on the scene is a company called Robin Hood. This company has a mobile app that can be used to trade on your smartphone or tablet. One advantage of Robin Hood is that it's commission free. It also allows you to invest in options and even cryptocurrencies, as well as directly in stocks.

Vanguard, a very popular investment firm known for mutual funds, also offers several ETF options. Their S&P 500 indexed fund VOO is one of the most popular investment options.

Another one of the big players in the ETF world is iShares by BlackRock. They are offered in four asset classes:

- Equity (stocks)
- Fixed income (bonds)
- Real estate
- Commodity

You can also invest by region:

- United States
- Europe
- Asia/Pacific
- Global

Or by market:

- Developed
- Emerging

For example, iShares offers a fund which tracks the Russell 2000. According to the website, had you invested $10,000 when the fund was started in 2000, today you've had about $40,000. The fund invests in smaller publicly traded U.S. companies that have long-term growth potential. Like investing in an S&P 500 index, this fund will give you a chance to invest simultaneously in all companies that make up the index – in this case, the 2000 small-cap companies on the Russell 2000.

If you look at the expense ratios, you see where you can get big advantages over a mutual fund. Expense ratios on iShares go as low as 0.04, with most around 0.19-0.20.

Remember these funds trade like stocks – so you don't have to enroll at iShares to buy iShares funds. You just have to know what the tickers are, and you can sign up with any brokerage firm and buy the funds as part of your everyday trades.

Note that while we've often talked about the S&P 500, you can invest in exchange-traded funds that track all markets. For example, the PowerShares QQQ fund tracks the NASDAQ 100.

The Advantages and Disadvantages

Although it's hard to say that ETFs have disadvantages, if you are person who would rather hand over control to a money manager, then an ETF is not for you because trading and investing in exchange-traded funds requires your active and direct participation, and there is no expert who is going to pick the right funds for you.

However, due to the instant and automatic diversification that exists with these types of investments, they are fairly low risk as long as you follow some basic investment common sense. The flexibility is a major advantage, but you shouldn't abuse it. In other words, when you decide to invest in a fund unless there is some very serious compelling reason to get out – stay in that fund. ETFs represent an opportunity for solid, long-term investing.

How to utilize ETFs and Where to Invest

You invest in ETFs at your regular brokerage. You should use the websites of major funds to educate yourself about what funds are on offer and what the goals are of each fund. That way you can carefully select funds that meet your own investment goals. You can also compare funds offered by one company versus another, to examine performance. SPDR also offers a small-cap fund that tracks the 2000 smallest publicly traded companies in the United States. How do the two funds compare?

- The iShares fund is larger, with 282 million outstanding shares, compared to about 40 million for the SPDR SPSM fund.
- Both have a similar P/E ratio of about 16.
- The expense ratio of the SPDR SPSM fund is 0.05%. For the iShares fund, it is 0.19%.
- The price of a share of SPSM is about $30, at the time of writing the iShares fund is $154 per share.
- Year to date, the iShares fund is up 15.8%, the SPSM fund is up 17.3%.

You might ask why the funds track the same index but don't offer the exact same performance. The reason is that each company makes its own decisions on the weight given for investments. For example, we can look at the top ten holdings of each fund. For the iShares fund we have:

- ETSY
- TRADE DESK INC-CLASS A
- FIVE BELOW INC
- CREE INC
- HUBSPOT
- PLANET FITNESS INC. CLASS A
- CIENA CORP.
- PRIMERICA INC.
- ENTEGRIS INC.
- ARRAY BIOPHARMA INC.

For SPDR's SPSM fund the top ten holdings are:

- MR. COOPER GROUP INC.
- TRADE DESK INCORPORATED CLASS A
- PLANET FITNESS CLASS A
- VERSUM MATERIALS INC.

- CREE INC.
- MELLANOX TECHNOLOGIES LTD.
- ITT
- ARRAY BIOPHARMA INC.
- COUPA SOFTWARE INC.
- INSPERITY INC.

As you can see, while there is some overlap, the different funds have given different weights to different companies, and the top ten lists then turn out different. The difference isn't all that significant, but you may note that the SPDR fund has performed a little better on a YTD basis. Over the past five years, the five-year market price of the SPDR fund has grown 7.59%, in comparison to 4.46% for the iShares fund. So the SPDR fund hasn't just done better recently, it is done better for the past five years. That coupled with its lower costs (both the share price and expense ratio) make it a more attractive option in our view. But we aren't here to advocate for one or the other, but rather to give you an idea of how you might do your own analysis with these types of funds. The lower share price of the SPDR fund will make it more accessible for those who are starting out with a lower budget or who don't want to risk large amounts of capital.

Super Diversification with ETFs

As we stated at the beginning and illustrated by looking at a couple of funds, ETFs provide automatic diversification, the same kind you get with mutual funds but without the costs, constraints, and hassles. If you want to build a solid, really diverse portfolio consider picking your favorite ETF company and buying into all of their funds over time, or a diverse subset of them. Since there are funds that invest in stocks, bonds, real estate, and commodities, it's pretty easy to build up a portfolio that meets your investment goals, whether you're playing it safe looking for an income-based portfolio or looking for aggressive growth or some balance in between.

ETFs versus Picking Stocks

ETFs trade like stocks, but they are not investments in individual companies.

Where did ETFs come from?

The history of exchange-traded funds traces its roots back through mutual funds. The first mutual fund was developed in 1774 by a Dutch merchant. At that time, he used pooled investing to allow people to invest in a closed-end fund. A closed-end fund has a pooled amount of capital that it raises through an IPO, and it's managed by a professional money manager. In modern times, closed-end funds are publicly traded funds themselves. From 1774 until modern times, mutual funds were the only game in town when it came to index funds.

The first attempt to launch an exchange-traded fund came in the United States in the late 1980s when there was a fund indexed to the S&P 500. However, a federal judge actually struck it down, saying the fund had to be traded in futures markets. This ruling kept the fund out of the reach of ordinary investors, but soon afterward the first true exchange-traded funds were brought to market.

In 1990, an exchange-traded fund was introduced on the Toronto stock exchange in Canada, which tracked 35 large Canadian companies. This was soon followed a few years later by the creation of the S&P 500 Trust, an ETF that was created by our friends the State Street Global Advisors SPDR. This fund caught fire and remains very popular today, and as we've seen, State Street has massively expanded the funds they have available with investing possibilities in virtually every asset class and market segment, both here in the United States and globally.

At first, ETFs were primarily used by institutional investors. However, their use quickly caught on, and financial advisors and individual investors became interested in using exchange-traded funds to invest. Between 2000 and 2010, the total amount invested in ETFs grew from $0.1 trillion to $1 trillion, and by 2017 that figure had grown to $3.4 trillion.

Chapter 7 Dividend Investing

What is Dividend Investing?

Dividend Investing is a term describing an approach in investment which entails purchasing stocks that have dividends. The main goal of Dividend investing is the generation of a stable passive income. Dividend investing is not as simple as its definition. There are intricacies involved. Luckily for you, this book equips you with ample knowledge to go about Dividend investing in your financial journey.
In this book, there will be frequent use of financial accounting terms. For those that are not in the finance field, this may make the reading of the book a little bit difficult to understand. However, here are some terms you should look out for in the course of reading. Knowing these terms should help simply their use as we move forward.

Stock: This term refers to a kind of security that equates proportionate ownership in the issuer company. Alternatively, a stock is called shares.

Dividend: This term is simply the portion of a company's profit paid to its shareholders. Dividends are not necessarily cash. They are in shares and other properties.

If you are not well convinced about dividend investing, it is time you stopped doubting the potentials of this investment strategy. There are many benefits of dividend investing, but, the accessible advantage that everyone will derive from is that it is an ideal source of retirement income. When you retire, you have the privilege to take some of your dividend payments and still retain ownership of stocks which will continually pay you for the rest of your life.

Why Invest in Dividend Stocks?

Notwithstanding the economic importance of dividend stocks, there are articles, books, reviews, and even experts' comments that discredit Dividend investing. As a result, many people are left undecided about the decision to invest in dividend stocks. "What if the company slashes the price of their dividends abruptly?"
"I read it up an article that the payment of dividends does not determine shares prices." These comments are some of the reasons why specific individuals are left undecided about the decision to invest in dividend stocks. Undoubtedly, nothing in this world has no pros and cons. The same principle applies to investment in dividend stocks. The good news about investing in dividend stocks is that the advantages greatly outweigh the cons. Besides, the few drawbacks of investing in dividend stocks should not make you lose a chance of a steady income. As an investor, if you want to make it financially, you must be willing to take a risk. Even if you choose not to invest in a dividend stock, there is a risk in your decision. You risk the chance of not benefiting from the earnings of dividend stocks.

Despite the few limitations of dividend stocks, there are countless reasons why you should invest in dividend stocks. So, to the big question:

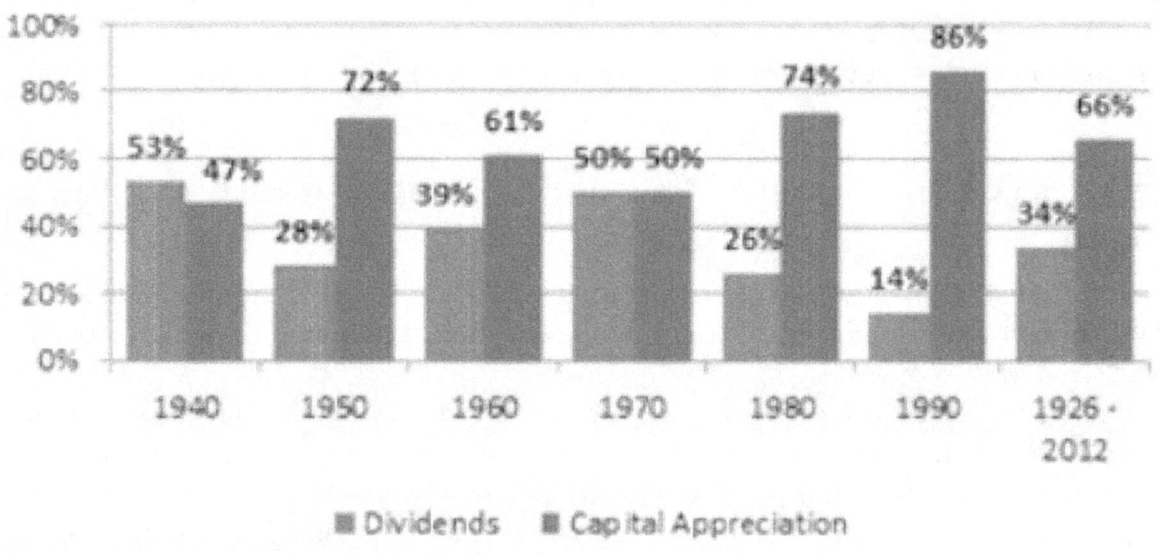

What Are the Benefits of Investing in Dividend Stocks?

Image showing the rate at which dividend investing can multiply your returns over time.

Dividend Stocks Investment Is an Avenue to Secure a Stable Stream of Income

One merit of dividend stock over other types of stocks is that it helps you achieve a source of passive income that is both steady and reliable. Unlike other forms of investments, you don't have to sell anything to make a profit.

When you invest in other types of stocks, you tend not to make a profit until you sell them. The set back of this characteristic is that you merely have a paper profit until you sell something. Yes, you make a profit. But the gain is only on paper as you are unable to cash out your rewards and earnings till you sell something. So, most investments are not ideal for a steady passive income.

The situation is different when you invest in dividend stocks. The primary thing that distinct dividend stocks from other investment options are that there are no paper profits. When you invest in Dividend investing, you have the assurance of cashing out raw and cold cash. There is no strict requirement to tell your broker to sell something when you are involved in Dividend investing.

Dividends are your earned money. Once paid, they cannot withdraw from you; this is the best part about investing in dividend stocks.

Also, the norm is that companies pay dividends frequently of a fiscal quarter (that is, every three months). If you are an investor seeking to multiply his/her income; dividend stocks, this is an investment option that you should consider. There is a guarantee for you to earn payment every three months. Say goodbye to financial inadequacy.

Investment in Dividend Stocks Translates to a Sufficient Income in the Retirement Period

When you invest in dividend stock for the long term, you're privileged to have a stable income when you retire. Here is a reason why you should invest in dividend stocks, and do so as soon as possible.

Research by several finance professionals shows that investors who build a dividend stock portfolio for the long term are more likely to acquire many shares when they age. The implication of having many Dividend-paying stocks at an old age or retirement period is that you have more than enough money to cater to your financial problems. You should invest in dividend-paying stocks because they are futuristic than their counterparts. When you buy dividend-paying stocks, you are confident in your decision, as you know that you are making a financial decision that guarantees financial freedom. Investing in dividend stocks brings you both short-term and long-term rewards.

For instance, a nurse named Jane makes steps towards securing her financial future by investing in dividend stocks by the time she is 40. If her dividend income is $50 at the time, with time, the income grows to $100 and continuously adds up. By the time she is 60, Jane's dividend income would have added up to $20,000 that rolls in equity. So, if you want to be like Jane, or even better, invest in dividend stocks.

Investment in Dividend Stocks Grants You the Privilege to Retain Your Shares and Ownership at the Same Time

Dividend stocks are not like other investment options. Typically, if you invest in a stock that does not pay a dividend, the only way for you to make money out of your shares is by selling them out. The implication of this is that you cannot make a profit and retain ownership of your shares. With ordinary shares, you cannot earn a profit while maintaining your stocks; you have to give in something for something, viz-a-viz.

The fear of losing ownership to gain profit is what pushes many people away from investing. They are incredibly skeptical of any form of investment due to their generalization of stocks. Not all stocks are the same. Dividend stocks, for instance, is significantly different from other types of stocks that do not pay dividends. Naturally, as humans, we are selfish, and we don't love losing out. Thus, we always want to gain. We don't accommodate the fear of making a loss; this is why some investors do not like the idea of selling shares. They are of the notion that selling their stocks in a company will affect them, especially in periods where growth is probable. So, people tend to reject the idea of investing in stocks as they believe earning profit makes them lose their source of income and ownership in a company.

As earlier stated, all stocks are not the same. The shares which prevent dual privilege of ownership and profitability are those that do not pay in dividends. Dividends paying stocks permits you to make money off your shares while still being in control of them. If you invest in dividend stocks, you do not have to fear the relinquishment of your ownership in a company.

With an investment in dividend stocks, you make a profit off your stocks while owning them for the possibility of capital appreciation.

Inflation Has Almost Nothing on Dividend Stocks

During inflation periods, your earnings are affected negatively. Despite the negative effect of inflation, you can keep your passive income safe from the negative impact that inflation hampers on the economy. When you invest in dividends paying stocks, you can WIN (Whip Inflation Now).

If you are a follower of history, then you are likely to remember that the WIN word came about in President Gerald Ford's administration. If you are ignorant about what happened, here is a quick recap. Back in August 1974, President Ford charged Americans to Whip Inflation Now (WIN) as there was a growing rate of inflation in the country then (about 11%). And the WIN strategy proved useful for most Americans as it provided a hedge against inflation.

Investment in dividend stocks protects your investment earnings from inflation; thus, if you are looking forward to ample protection in inflation periods. If you want to smile while others are crying wolf, invest in dividend stocks.

A significant benefit of dividends over most income-generating investments is that they can keep pace with the rate of inflation. Dividend stock prices increase as the general price level in an economy increases. When prices inflate, companies gain more profit. The increased earnings of companies permit them to increase the rates of dividend payments. Consequently, you make more profit as an investor. However, inflation still takes a bite out of your investment income as a modest 3% inflation has the potential to reduce the 7% on your annual earnings to a meager sum of 4%.

Investing in Dividend Stocks Provides a Win-Win Opportunity

Most investment generating options do not allow you to win totally. For instance, you are an investor solely in ordinary shares that do not pay in dividends; you are likely to succeed in only one way. The only way that you can win is if you sell the stock at a high price. Ironically, you suffer a more significant loss as instability is almost synonymous with Wall Street (stock exchange market). There is no surety that share prices will increase to an amount that earns you profit. Even if a while is stable, the stability is often short-lived due to frequent fluctuations of shares value. Therefore, there is a probability that you may lose in two ways when you invest in ordinary shares. You drop in profitability at regular intervals, and more importantly, you lose the ownership of your stocks.

The situation of things is a little bit better when you invest in dividend stocks. While you are subject to the same culture of the instability of Wall Street, you are more secure when you invest in dividends stocks. Unlike other types of shares, dividends provide the win-win option. You have considerably stable ownership of your stocks while making money from it in your possession. If the issuing corporation pays you your dividend check and your stock value increase at the same time, you make terrific money from income and capital appreciation. If you don't want to earn your dividend immediately, you can reinvest it to buy more stocks.

As earlier stated, Wall Street is not all bed of roses. You can equally lose out when you invest in dividend stocks. Investing in dividend stocks does not give you immunity from frequent loss. But you are safer than when you rely only on shares that do not reward in dividends.

There Is Better Security in Dividend Investing as Issuing Companies Are Strong Performers

The issuing companies contribute significantly to the success of an investment. One good thing about investing in dividends is that there are always good stocks included in the stock portfolio. The main reason why there are still excellent and profitable stocks in dividend stocks is that companies issuing dividends stocks have a great financial capacity. Thus, they are capable of distributing to their investors without difficulty. Most companies that permit dividends stock purchases in their companies are mostly stable and reputable performers. An example of a company that is an active performer is Coca-Cola. Coca-Cola pays 3.5% in dividends annually.

According to a Forbes article written in 2015, dividend stocks have consistently improved in performance between 1927 to 2014. The article also reports that Dividend-paying stocks are profitable than non-dividend paying stocks as the former averagely paid 10.4% annually; while the latter paid 8.5% annually during the stipulated period. These stats show the fact that dividend stocks perform better than any other income-generating investment in the long run. The quality delivery of dividend stocks is attributable to issuing companies' strong performance.

There is always better security guaranteed when you invest in dividend stocks. As an investor, you are confident in the issuing company's reputation not to disappoint. Thus, you invest without fears of the unknown which other investment options expose you. Although dividend issuing companies experience a severe downturn in business at times, this instance is scarce.

Invest in dividend stocks if you want an investment option that has reduced risks, better security, and higher earning potentials.

Investing in Dividend Stocks Allows You to Exploit Bear Markets and Corrections

When you invest in dividend stocks, you are privileged to take advantage of bear markets and corrections period. If you invest in dividends paying a share, you can take advantage of the momentary falls in stock prices.

When bear market situations occur, and there is a fall of stock pricing, no doubt, your investment earnings are affected. With an investment in stocks that pay dividends, the bear market and corrections will turn out to be a potential earning opportunity for you. If you are smart enough as an investor, you will invest in shares a lot during the bear and corrections period. These investments pay in the long run when the prices recover back to their original form as returns on investments increasingly enhance.

You should invest in dividend stocks because there is an opportunity to boost dividend returns during crucial periods such as bear markets.

When You Invest in Dividend Stocks, You Become Free from the Complexities of the Market

A typical behavior exemplified by most investors is the frequent questioning of where the market is heading. The truth is that no one, including knowledgeable investors, have the omniscient knowledge of the market's direction. The market is unpredictable and constantly evolving. The dynamism of the stock market makes most non-investors doubt the sureness of the stock market to be profitable. Since prices are always rising, how does one become protected from the negative impact of these fluctuations?

Fortunately, dividend stocks seem to be the answer. As an investor in dividend stocks, you automatically get unhooked from the market and its uncertainties. In similarity to a worker waiting for a regular paycheck; you rest assured that you will receive regular earnings from the issuing corporations. While other investors who have investments in ordinary shares fall as victims of the changing market, you remain safe as your portfolio's income remains steady. The best part about all of these is that at times where prices are uncertain, the issuing companies might luckily increase the dividends that they payout. If you are skeptical about this reason because a company might go insolvent, bear in mind that you will still receive income in such a situation. Dividend stocks give you peace of mind as the happenings of the market do not entirely determine your income.

Dividend Stocks Have Some Tax Advantages

There are two types of dividends: qualified dividends and non-qualified dividends. Unlike non-qualified dividends, available profits are less taxed. Qualified dividends taxes are at a rate that is below the marginal rate. The implication of this is that whenever you earn money from qualified dividends, your earnings' taxes will be lower as their charges are at a long-term capital gains rate. Thus, if you seek a way to escape the claws of taxes, you should consider the option of investing in dividend stocks, especially stocks with qualified dividends.

Note that the special status of qualified dividends is not definite unless Congress confers a permanent state that makes them tax-favored. So, there is a probability that earned dividends might revert to being taxed at a marginal rate, similar to the marginal rate. The fantastic thing about dividend stocks is that it provides you with other options when one fails. With dividend-paying stocks, there is a way. Dividend stocks have an alternative method of making you enjoy tax advantages as you are permitted to keep your stocks in tax-advantaged accounts. As an investor in dividend shares, you have the luxury to keep your stocks in your 401 (k), IRAA, or probably your health savings account. You should apply carefulness in how you go about saving in the listed accounts. There might be complications along the way.

The reasons why you should invest in the listed accounts are numerous. For one, when you transfer your dividends to a traditional account, you'll be mandated to pay the regular income tax at your peculiar marginal rate during withdrawal. If you want to keep your investment taxes from the ordinary income tax rate, then keep them in a Roth IRA. A Roth IRA is an account that allows you to save your retirement income without being taxed). Through this method, you gain a steady passive income for yourself and also secure your financial future. Alternatively, you can keep your dividends in your 401 (k) or HSA (Health Savings Account) depending on the intended purpose. By doing these, you smartly avoid taxes on your dividends.

With Dividend Reinvesting, You Can Maximize Returns Optimally

By now, it should not come as a surprise to you that investing in dividend stocks has a lot of advantages. Now, imagine the benefits that reinvestment in dividend stocks will generate. Yes, reinvesting in dividend stocks has better advantages; it merely multiples the effect of a single dividend's investment.

You should start investing in dividend stocks because it is through that you can reinvest in the first place. A reinvestment in dividends paying stocks is an effective method that you can use to exploit the benefits of the compounding.

Reinvesting your dividends multiplies your returns at a geometric rate. With a reinvestment in dividends, you can effortlessly supercharge the returns on your earnings. If you are an investor in dividend-paying stocks in the U.S. index, you will multiply your profits at a geometric rate of 198x, if you invest for capital gains. What a profitable venture you might say. Nevertheless, reinvesting your dividends lets you gain 8,400 higher your returns. I hear you mutter, *amazing!*

You can tap into the unbelievable benefit of dividend investing, decide to start investing in dividend stocks today.

Chapter 8 Financial Planning

What is Financial Planning?

Financial planning can be defined as the elaborate process and procedures of developing financial policies and making estimates of capital requirements for purposes of investing, procurement, and administration. There are a number of objectives that necessitate financial planning. Companies undertake financial planning basically in search of one of the following objectives.

Determination of Capital Requirements

There are various ways of establishing the capital requirements of any venture. This mostly depends on expected costs and expenses such as the costs for fixed and current assets, marketing costs, and so on. Such costs and expenses have to be viewed both in the short and long term.

Financial Policies Framing

We also undertake financial planning for purposes of framing financial policies especially when it comes to borrowing, lending, and for purposes of financial control.

Also, finance managers of officers are tasked with ensuring that finances, which are a scarce commodity, are prudently spent and utilized in the most effective and best possible way. This way, companies are able to maximize the returns on their investments.

What is a Financial Plan?

A financial is essentially a comprehensive statement regarding an investor's long-term outlook and objectives. These objectives include personal wellbeing, financial security, and detailed investments and savings strategies. Such a plan can be created by an investor or with the aid of a financial advisor. You should come up with a plan that suits your ambitions and meets your investment desires.

It is important that you understand the entire financial planning process. This is because you will need to apply these principles in designing your investing strategy. The initial step is always coming up with the contents of the plan. Therefore, you will need to get pen and paper then put down all the aspects that you consider important. Financial plans can be crafted for a number of reasons. Some of these are listed below.

- Determining cash flow

- Calculating your net worth

- Long-term investment plan

- Tax reduction strategy

- Retirement plan

Please note that there is no single template designed to come up with a financial plan. In short, we can conclude that a financial plan is a strategy that details an individual's investment goals and writes down the strategy in a sequential manner. The plan should outline the objective of the investment or whatever other financial undertaking the individual wishes to undertake. The plan should start with a person's net worth or the amount of funds available for investment purposes.

Investing versus Trading

All traders usually engage in active trading. Active trading simply means selling and buying of securities on a regular basis based on price movement for fast and easy profits. This is as opposed to buying then holding like investors do. Buy-and-hold strategy is a long-term strategy where investors hope to capitalize on eventual share price gain.

As a trader, you will engage in active trading in highly liquid markets searching for profitable opportunities based on price movements on certain stocks and shares. The most commonly traded securities are stocks even though there is a wider option available.

As a trader, you will need to be a lot more speculative compared to the average investor which leads us to the use of fundamental and technical analysis. Technical analysis will come in handy when you plan your trades. You will also require additional tools including price charts which are crucial tools for any active trader.

You will need to make a lot of trades if you are to be profitable. High trade volumes are recommended with volatility. As a trader, you should find volatile stocks with large volumes and plenty of price movement. The reason why you should deal in high volume stocks is that price movements are often small so to maximize profits, large volumes are necessary.

Another important aspect of active trading includes the regular application of limit orders. These orders enable you the trader to determine and set stock prices ideal for selling your stocks. As a trader, you need to plan your trades so that you know when to take profits and what points to exit a trade. To exit a non-performing trade, you will need to define stop-loss points.

A stop-loss order is an order that you come with to prevent your trades from losing you money. A typical stop-loss order identifies a price point located at a lower position on the trend. Should the price fall to the stop-loss point then you will automatically exit the trade and prevent further loss of funds. This point is considered the maximum loss that you can take per trade. It is advisable to take this approach as you risk letting your emotions get the better of you.

Sometimes traders, especially inexperienced and novice traders, let emotions get the better of their trades. In some instances they are scared of losing money and so they exit trades at the slightest price pullback. Others allow the price to fall astronomically thinking they will recoup their money later. They end up losing large amounts of their trading capital. This is a wrong approach that should be avoided at all costs.

You trades should be based on your analysis and not emotions. You need to sit down and take time to plan and work out your trades. Use all the tools at your disposal to chart your pathway. Along the path you will need to identify a take-profit point as well as a stop-loss point. If you do your analysis properly and learn how to execute trades the correct way, then you will not need to let emotions take charge. Instead you will allow your trades to execute per the plan to conclusion. This is a more stable, more profitable, and the only recommended approach to active trading.

This way, you will be able to trade without having to watch your trades closely. In rare cases, you may want to intervene. For instance, if you collect the profits and the market continues on a bull run, you do not need to exit right away. You can first collect profit and let your trade continue on with the winning trend. However, you should work out and define new take-profit and exit points. These will ensure that your trades remain profitable until the trend changes direction.

Similarities between Investing and Trading

Trading and investing have plenty of similarities. Both a trader and an investor have a common goal of generating an income and then investing the same as is required. Investors often buy long positions and then hold for a while. Active investing therefore refers to all activities pertaining to stock's future.

Traders prefer taking short-term market positions so they can exit quickly when the time comes. This is as opposed to investors who love long-term positions and can remain in a position for longer periods of time. As an active investor, you will mostly be seeking alpha. The term alpha is used in finance to indicate a strategy where a trader wins in the market and makes a profit. It can also be considered as a measure of performance.

In the case above, we can deduce alpha to imply the difference between the returns received from a securities portfolio and a benchmark or index. Basically, actively traded portfolios are deemed to perform better in some cases compared to passively traded ones.

Risk and Volatility

Investing is wrought with risks and they can happen at any time. As an investor you need to be aware that you will be facing different types of risks at all times. In fact, the only investments thought to be without risk are fixed income assets like bonds.

Fortunately risks can be managed. There are some risks that you can handle but there are others that are beyond your control. You can only guard against those beyond your control. However, as an investor, you need to determine your risk level and if you do this correctly, then you investment risks will remain at generally acceptable levels.

There are certain risks that we can do nothing about. These are risks that perhaps affect an entire industry and sometimes even the whole market. Such risks demand investors to take certain actions such as adjust their portfolios or simply ride out and weather the storm.

There are certain risks that are considered major by the investing community. They can be categorized into four distinct groups. Fortunately, finance experts have invented ways of managing these risks so they have minimal effect on your investments.

Risks Posed by the General Economy

The general economy poses a major risk to investments because it can tank at any time. Think about the terror attacks of 2001 and the market crunch of 2007. All these pose a huge risk to investments and if not properly managed could cause huge losses. When the economy falls, most indexes follow suit and it takes them months to recover. Therefore, always be wary of the general economy. When the economy is doing well, then your investments will follow suit and will thrive. However, the reverse is also true because a falling economy will drag down the value of the stock market.

If you are a young investor, then one of the options you have is to wear out or ride out the economic downturn. Such moments are the best to buy into a solid company. Think about blue chip companies. If you are able to buy into strong companies such as major banks, telecommunication firms, multinationals, and so on, then you will be able to weather the storms and emerge even better than before.

However, some economic situations might be just too major such that there is nothing anyone can do about it. Think about the economy collapse of 2008 caused by the sub-prime mortgage market. Plenty of investors lost huge chunks of their investments. It has taken ages to recover from that economic disaster. If you are an older investor, then it is advisable to begin transferring most of your investments to fixed income securities and bonds. Fortunately such incidents are rare, few, and far between.

Risks Due to Inflation

We also have risks posed by inflation. Inflation can be viewed as a tax on all consumers. However, inflation is defined generally as the sustained increase in the price of goods and services within an economy. This means that costs are always going up and this affects plenty of things. As an investor, inflation might affect your investments and reduce the value. Most of the time, the government is able to keep inflation under control. However, in some instances, government borrowing and programs tend to introduce inflation.

To evade the effects of inflation, investors tend to put their money in commodities such as gold and other precious metals as well as real estate. However, stocks are thought to be the best protection against inflation. This is because companies are able to adjust prices to beat inflation.

Risk to Market Value

This kind of risk is what can happen should the market move against your investment. This usually occurs when the market changes its usual trend and pursues other interests such as the next big thing. Think about the technology bubble of the 90s. Back then, a lot of traders abandoned traditional stocks and pursued tech stocks instead. This had a huge effect on ordinary investments and investors had to make quick adjustments.

On rare occasions the market may collapse with the net effect of devaluing both bad and good stocks. While this may harms some investors, others have learnt to view it positively. They consider this as the best time to buy into strong companies.

Being too Conservative

Investors can sometimes be too conservative. While this is not necessarily a bad thing, it can have negative consequences if carried out to near extremes. Investors who never take risks and simply wish to play it safe may not achieve their financial goals. Remember the stock market is all about investing. As such, you need to take calculated albeit small risks occasionally. If you perform your analysis accurately, then you will emerge the winner most of the time. Therefore, avoid saving up large amounts of money in your savings account and put it in meaningful investments at the stock markets.

Volatility and Investments

The stock market is mostly a very volatile place. Swings tend to happen on a quarterly, annual, and daily basis for indexes such as the Dow Jones Industrial Average. Volatility left unchecked can cause serious damage to investments. However, if properly harnesses, it can grow your investments significantly and generate great value especially if you learn how to take advantage of it.

What is Volatility?

Volatility is defined as a measure of spread or dispersion across the average or mean returns of a financial asset. It can also be measured through the standard deviation. This basically indicates how close to the mean that a commodity's price is. When prices are generally closer together, then the standard deviation is smaller and widespread prices indicate a larger standard deviation.
In short, we can deduce that volatility at the stocks market is closely linked to investment risk even though it can be harnessed for profitability. To measure volatility we use standard deviation. Standard deviation is an indicator of how closely a security's price is clustered close to the moving average. It is advisable to learn some techniques of harnessing volatility in order to benefit significantly from it.

Shorting Stocks and Winning

A lot of investors view stocks as a sort of game which can be played to win. This means that the stock market is viewed as a platform and stocks are instruments which can be used to generate profits. As such, tactical investors can play the game of stocks and win. We understand profits to mean buying stocks at low prices and selling at higher prices. However, this is a simplistic approach and investors can do much better.

Short Selling

One approach to winning at the markets is through short selling. Investors use shorting either to minimize losses or sometimes to generate profits. However, there are others who view shorting negatively and perceive it to be a risky affair. Sometimes investors choose to short-sell a company's stock when they believe a strategy will work or conditions are ripe.

What Does Shorting a Stock Mean?

Basically, investors buy stocks at a low price and believe the price will eventually rise and they will be able to sell at a higher price for a profit. This is a common strategy and is usually referred to as going long on a stock. It is especially useful when an investor believes a certain stock will increase in value in the coming days or even weeks.

On the other hand, when a stock is about to lose value, then traders prefer to sell it before buying it back and making a profit. If an investor believes that certain stocks will fall in price in the coming days, they will sell them off at market rates and wait for the price to fall before purchasing them back. This is usually a risky affair and more so because the shares or stocks often belong to others. Short selling simply means selling stocks that you do not own.

If the strategy works then the investor stands to make a neat profit. However, if it flops then the losses could be disastrous. In fact traders and investors both claim the losses could be unlimited. This is because the price of the sold shares could rise to unbelievably high levels.

Example - Short Selling

Now an investor reads up some business and finance news and believes that stocks of company ABC will fall because of certain factors. The investor is so sure of this that he decides to act. Most other investors would not touch this stock for fear of losing money. However, the short-seller is very interested. So he chooses to act.

ABC shares are currently trading at $100 per share. The investor decides to borrow 100 shares from his broker. He then sells these shares for a total amount of $10,000. As predicted, the share price falls in a couple of weeks' time and trade at $80. The investor decides to buy them back and spends a total of $80 * 100 = $8,000. The short selling process earns him a cool $2,000. However, this is not always the case and sometimes investors lose money trying to profit from shorting stocks.

The Strategy

There are three different ways of profiting from the short sale approach. Firstly, you can choose to sell stocks short in any liquid market that is devoid of any special restrictions. Also, the security to be traded must be held by a broker or any other individual but the investor needs access to the shares. However, it is very common to come across issues of naked short sales devoid of any corresponding inventory. This is mostly attributed to competition at the markets.

Chapter 9 Setting Goals

It is crucial to set investing goals. This will help the investor to recognize what they are willing to put into their investing, as well as which investing methods are the best for them. If hiring an advisor, it is important to make them aware of the goals of the investor. There are several aspects of stock investing that the investor should be aware of their goals in. The individual should decide what period that they wish to invest in. They must also decide how much time each week they wish to devote to trading. Another important aspect to consider is how much the investor is willing to invest, both initially and regularly. One must consider how much risk they are willing to undertake. There should be some sort of goal with how much growth is desired, so that the investor's progress may be monitored and adjusted if needed.

Time Period

Investors should consider how long they are willing to invest their money. Some wish to hold onto their investments for a long period of time, utilizing the "buy and hold" strategy. Others prefer to buy stock and trade that same stock within the day or a few days. Some wish to purchase stock as a way to invest in their retirement. The time period that is best for the investor will depend on the investor, their goals, and their financial situation. For those who will need the money that they have invested, a shorter-term investment plan may seem more appealing. Others may choose to set aside a bit of money each month to put towards building stock for the long-term.

For those wishing to choose a lower-risk option, long-term investment is wise. This is because short-term losses will be offset by long-term gains, as the stock market tends to stabilize itself and rise and the long-term. Some may be using the stock as an alternative to a savings account and will later need access to that money. Perhaps one wishes to buy a house in two and a half years using part of the money from their stock investments. This will give the investor up to two and a half years to continue with the investment of that money.

The amount of time that the investor is willing to keep their money in stock is known as the time horizon. For instance, the time horizon for the individual who wishes to buy a house in two and a half years would be two and a half years. Before investing, the future investor should truly consider what time period that they are able to invest. They should consider whether or not they will need the money that they plan to invest at a future date and when that date is. They should also consider what they are saving towards or what their investing goal is. This will help to determine the best time period for their investment. It should also be noted whether or not there will be further money added to the investment. If so, the investor should know when the money will be added and how much will be added.

The ideal time period will vary from investor to investor. The time period will also affect other factors of the investment, such as the amount of risk that the investor should be willing to take. It may also affect the amount of time that the investor must dedicate to trading stocks.

Time to Devote to Trading

For some, trading is their primary source of income. Others may enjoy trading stock as a side hobby. There are even individuals that buy a stock only to hold onto it and essentially forget about it. Investors may choose to spend as much or as little time as they would like on their stock investments. There are several aspects of trading that require the investor to dedicate additional time to. There is education, research, trading, and management/diversification. All of these activities must be accounted for when the trader is considering how much time they are willing to spend on stock.

Before even starting out, investors must educate themselves. It is crucial to the investor's success to educate themselves on the stock market. One must familiarize themselves with all of the options that the stock market may offer them before jumping into any investment. This will help them to recognize which type of investments and strategies may best work for them and their goals. Otherwise, the investor is risking missed opportunities when it comes to investing. They must also research which stockbroker will best fit their needs. There may be one that has fewer fees, is easier for them to navigate, and offers optimal customer service. There are a number of terms that may help the investor to understand the stock market more effectively.

Investing in stock also requires great research. The investor must first educate themselves on the economy and how it works to understand the patterns of it better. They may also be able to identify better elements of the economy that will allow them to predict the movement of the economy. This may prove significant for short-term investments. It will also help the investor to identify better times to buy the stock. Day traders must study the market for hours each day. It may also help to construct charts and graphs to understand better and display the direction of the market. For these traders, it is necessary to dedicate that much time to research. Greater research will lead to greater returns. It is best for the trader to dedicate time to a number of resources to gain a better understanding of stock and be able to study multiple resources that are also studying the economy.

The investor must also conduct the actual trading. This takes a bit of time, as the investor must choose which stock they wish to purchase and sell. They must also decide how much stock they would like to purchase. This may take a bit of time; however, trading is made quite simple and quick now that most transactions are located online.

There must also be time dedicated to managing and diversifying the stockholder's portfolio. Without diversification, the investor is risking a heavy loss in their investments. Diversification allows the investor to experience losses in some areas yet make up for those losses with gains in other areas. The investor must regularly manage their portfolio. This may require writing down each of their investments or creating charts and graphs that depict their portfolio. This may show which areas may need balancing to ensure that the portfolio is properly diversified. The investor must regularly check to ensure that they are working towards their goals by trading the proper amount.

How Much to Invest

The investor must decide how much they are willing to invest. They should only invest money that they will not need in the near future. Long-term investing is the key to growing money, not saving money. Short-term investing is typically for a quick profit, yet there is the risk of losing that money. For that reason, the investor must be careful not to risk all of their money that they will need for the future. To decide how much money the investor is willing to invest will require planning. It is quite helpful to write down how much money the individual currently has total, including savings and investments. The individual should also account for all regular expenses, including but not limited to bills, groceries, gas, and entertainment. Additionally, the individual should consider how much money they earn each month (or whichever time period desired). They should also consider any current savings goals. Based on this information, the individual may start out with their total money currently. They should decide the best use of this money and make any necessary changes. Then, the individual should take their earnings and subtract necessary spending money (creating a budget for themselves). This way, the individual "pays themselves" first and has money left over to distribute appropriately. This remaining money may be used for saving or investing, depending on the goals of the individual. Each time period, the individual should follow the plan that they set for themselves to successfully invest the proper amount of money to achieve their goals. Additionally, the investor should decide how much stock to invest in. Perhaps their goal is buying 100 shares of Company A and 50 shares of Company B. They may develop a 10-week plan, purchasing 10 shares of Company A and 5 of Company B each week. Perhaps the investor wishes to buy 240 shares of 10 companies over the course of two years. They may buy 10 shares of each company every month for those two years. There may also be monetary goals, such as working towards owning one million dollars' worth of stock over the course of several years. Whatever the goals are of the investor, there should be a set time period, set amount of companies that they wish to invest in, and a set monetary amount or share amount that the investor wishes to invest in (it may be easier to set the number of shares, as the monetary value of the stocks will fluctuate). This will ensure that the investor sets a measurable goal for themselves. It is much easier to set an ultimate goal and split it up into smaller goals. The investor may even keep a notebook for their investments and write down their goals for each week.

Risk

The investor must also how much risk they are comfortable with taking. This will be strongly affected by the other goals that the investor sets. An investor that is more educated and dedicates more time studying the market will be more comfortable with taking more risk, as their market predictions will likely be more accurate as of the result of further education and knowledge. An investor that has more to invest will be more willing to risk more, especially if they diversify their portfolio. The investor may easily dedicate a certain percentage of their investments to high-risk stocks, a certain percentage to medium-risk stocks, and the remaining percentage to low-risk stocks. An investor will also be more willing to invest in higher-risk stocks if the money that they are investing isn't necessary (it won't be needed in the near future, and the investor can afford to lose this money if necessary). There is also a somewhat inverse relationship between risk and dividends. An investor that is primarily focused on earning dividends will not be as concerned with selecting a stock that they believe will increase drastically in the future (although that is certainly an added bonus). High-risk stock that is predicted to increase drastically in the future typically doesn't give its stockholders a high dividend; however, there are always exceptions.

Growth and risk tend to be directly related. The more an investor wishes to experience growth, the more they must (usually) be willing to risk. Penny stocks, which are very affordable stocks, are typically bought in bulk with the hope that their value will multiply over time. However, these are usually high-risk investments, as these are typically companies that are just starting out. The more well-established companies will typically experience more stability, whereas these companies tend to be highly volatile.

Those who don't wish to diversify their portfolio are increasing their risk. For those who wish to only invest in one company or sector, there is a much greater risk. If that company or sector fails, there is nothing to fall back on. However, one may decrease their risk by diversifying their portfolio. That way, losses in one area may be offset by gains in another. For investors that wish to only invest in one area, though, there will be higher risk in their investments. This is a personal preference, and it is up to the investor to decide what their course of action is.

How Much Growth Desired

Much like the investor should decide how much they wish to start off with investing, they should plan how much growth they desire. Coming up with a measurable goal will help to make this easier. The investor should set goals for either each stock or their portfolio as a whole. Perhaps the investor will sell the stock when they have reached double the original value. There may also be a certain dollar threshold the stockholder wishes to reach before they sell the stock. On the other hand, the investor may wish to simply hold onto their stock and enjoy the dividends that they receive. There may not be a desire for mass growth. However, the investor shouldn't completely neglect growth; it is still crucial.

Although not every investor is highly concerned with massive growth, it is still crucial to understand the goals of the individual as far as growth is concerned. An investor who desires high growth in a short amount of time must increase their level of risk in the investments that they make. Investors who desire high growth must also (typically) put in more time into researching their investments properly. By doing so, they will be able to better select well-performing stocks. Those who invest more will experience greater growth, monetary, than those who make the same decisions but with less money. If a stock grows by 10%, the investor who bought $50,000 of that stock will yield a much higher return than the investor who bought $7,000 of it (assuming that all other factors are the same). The percentage is the same, yet the return is higher.

There are several ways to measure growth, and each investor will have their own goals regarding growth. Some investors wish to reach a certain percentage of their original investment, and then they will be willing to sell that stock. Others wish to reach a certain monetary amount before they are willing to sell their stock. Other investors don't have a certain point in growth that they desire; they have a time period that they desire to keep their stock for (such as for retirement) and simply want to make the most that they can. Some investors value growth over risk; others wish to keep their risk low, sacrificing the opportunity for additional growth.

The investor should regularly document how much their stock has grown to ensure that they are achieving their goals. If they are below their desired growth rate, adjustments may have to be made. The investor should, however, consider that stock is volatile. Nonetheless, it is important always to track one's progress to ensure that they are meeting and exceeding their personal goals. This will ensure the greatest success to the investor and ensure the greatest possible return on the investor's money.

Portfolio Diversification

The investor should decide how diverse that they would like their portfolio to be. Perhaps the investor only wishes to invest in one or two stocks and dedicate all of their investments to that area. Perhaps the investor wishes to buy a multitude of stocks in a variety of sectors. This is up to personal preference, although it may be influenced by and serve as an influence of other factors. If the right stock is selected, concentrating all of one's investments into one stock may be the right choice for the highest yield. To minimize risk, diversification is crucial. Those who desire a more long-term investment may opt for higher diversification, as the performance of different sectors may vary over the long-term. Investors who are able and willing to dedicate more time to investing will be more able to properly diversify their stock investments, as they will be able to properly research and gain knowledge on a number of stocks, as opposed to specializing in and focusing on one. Those who don't wish to or aren't able to invest a great amount may benefit from diversification, as they won't experience as much loss in the case of a sector-specific or stock-specific loss.

It is important to set goals for how many shares of stock that the investor desires to purchase over time. The investor may also set a monetary goal for the stock. They may either set a goal for specific stocks or for a certain sector. By doing so, they are ensuring proper diversification for their needs and wants. By regularly ensuring that they are keeping up with and exceeding their goals, the investor is allowing for maximum success in their investments.

Investing vs. Saving vs. Debt

The individual should take a look at their finances and determine the best course of action for their needs and goals. The easiest way to do so is first to select goals for what the individual wants to save up for or save up to. This will give the individual direction. After that, any debt should be accounted for. This is the priority before investing unless the yield of the investment outweighs the percentage of the debt. For instance, a credit card payment with a 2% interest is a lower priority than stock that yields a 10% return. If the numbers were switched, the debt should be fully repaid before investing. Although the credit card debt must still be repaid, the focus should not be solely on that repayment; if possible, extra money may go into stock instead of all extra money going towards that repayment.

After the debt is accounted for, the current money supply of the individual should be accounted for and properly disbursed into savings and investing. This allocation will vary based on the person. After this, the person's income minus expenses (bills, entertainment, gas, etc.) should be calculated. This number will reveal the regular amount of "free" money that the individual will possess. This money should go towards savings or investing, depending on the individual's goals. There should definitely be a good amount of money in savings (about three months' worth of income), and the rest may be put into investing. However, there are exceptions to the rule. If the individual does not wish to risk investing their money and has a specific savings goal, they should work towards that as well. If the individual does not have enough money yet to invest, they should either find a way to increase their income, decrease their expenses, or better balance the money they are dispersing into savings and investing.

It is crucial for the investor to set goals for themselves. This will serve as a guide to the investor as to how much to invest, how much risk to take, how much growth to aim for, how much the portfolio must be diversified, and how to decide what to do with the investor's money.

Choosing a Broker

Once you've done all your preparation, the next step is to choose a broker so that you can start trading. In the old days, choosing a broker meant going to an office where an actual stockbroker worked. Today, a "broker" is usually an online website or even a mobile app, and everything is run by computer. The role of a broker is to buy and sell shares for you and manage your account. Brokers can also lend you money that you can use to buy shares or options, or they can lend you shares. There are various factors to consider when selecting a broker, including commissions and fees, features, and tools offered by their websites and the level of personal service provided. Choosing a broker is a personal decision and motivated largely by taste, so we cannot tell you which broker to select. You can go online and search for brokers or brokerages and find one that works best for you. In this chapter, we'll consider the factors that you should use when making your selection.

The Role of a Broker

The broker plays the role of a middleman. You will place your orders with the broker to buy or sell stocks, and the broker will actually carry out the transaction for you. They will also maintain your account and keep records for you, including anything you'll need related to your investing for tax purposes.

Brokers also provide many investment tools, although the offerings will vary. Some brokers provide a complete suite of tools that let you chart stocks, study past behavior, and review financial statements. Many brokers even offer simulators that people interested in trading can use to hone their skills. Whether or not you actually need these tools in your account is questionable, since there are many free resources available online. However, some people like to have all of their tools in one location.

Brokers can also play the role of a lender. You can borrow money or even borrow shares. The money can't be used for any purpose, the money would remain in your brokerage account, and you can use it to purchase shares of stock and other financial securities. Borrowing money from the broker to buy shares is known as "trading on the margin."

1. *Full Service vs. Discount Brokers*

Generally, brokers can be classified as either being full service or discount brokers. A full-service broker goes beyond simply providing the tools and computer interface to trade stocks. They will actually make investment advice available to their clients. A full-service broker is more in line with what you probably think of when you say the word "stockbroker." An example would be Charles Schwab or Fidelity.

Discount brokers, on the other hand, are largely automated and found online. These firms only provide the mechanics you will use in order to buy your shares and maintain your account. Some may provide educational information, and in the case of tasty works (to use one example) that information can be quite extensive, including full video suites of tutorials. Others, like Robinhood, provide minimal sets of tools and limited information, but the trade off is they are very simple to use.

The bottom line with your choice here is that if you want access to a financial advisor to help you make your investment decisions, then you're going to want to go with a full-service broker. If you are comfortable being an independent investor and are completely comfortable going it alone, then you can use a discount broker. Of course, nothing is free, so you should expect higher fees from a full-service broker.

Commissions and Fees

Commissions and fees are tacked on to your trades, and depending on how much you trade, they can add up. If you're a frequent trader, that means they can be a consideration when thinking about your profitability. Some brokerages charge small or even zero commissions. An example of this is Robinhood, which has become popular among amateur options traders for that reason along with its simplicity of use. Options only last from one week to a month in most cases, so people who trade options will be making frequent trades, and they don't want commissions eating into their profits.

An organization like Charles Schwab or Fidelity that may make professional financial advisors available to you is probably going to charge higher commissions, in order to pay for the service.

Account Minimums

Different brokerages are going to have different account minimums. Some will even let you open an account without depositing any money. But others may require that you deposit a significant amount of funds just to get started. If you are starting out small and this is an issue for you, then you need to shop around and make sure you open an account with a brokerage that has no account minimums.

Broker Recommendations

If you decide to go with a full-service broker, you might utilize them to help you with your stock picks. For people that feel more comfortable having a trained professional assist you with this task, it may be worth the higher commissions. You might want to read reviews on firms that you are considering in order to determine whether or not they have a good track record. A minimal requirement would be to see if their recommendations meet the S & P 500 benchmark, but you will probably want advisement from someone who can actually beat it. If you decide to discuss your investments with an advisor, you should have your financial goals clearly set in your mind before doing so. That means being able to tell them your time horizon and investment goals (growing wealth rapidly, income investing, etc.). You will also need to have some idea about how much you plan to invest and what your plans are for a future investment schedule. If you find that their recommendations are not to your liking, you are not required to follow them. But they may attempt to pressure you to do so.

Asset Classes and Types of Brokerage Accounts

Different brokerages may allow investment in different asset classes or markets. If you are interested in going beyond simple stock investing, and engaging in activities like trading options or investing directly in bonds, you are going to need to investigate what your broker does and does not allow. To get exactly what you need, you may have to open more than one brokerage account. For example, some people may be interested in investing in stocks but also engaging in Forex or crypto trading. Finding one broker that does all you want may be possible, but you might have to open other accounts for more specialized trading.

There are two major types of brokerage accounts. A cash account is a standard account. That is, you deposit cash from your bank, and then you buy shares using the cash in the account. If you want to buy more shares, you have to deposit more money.

The other type of brokerage account is a margin account. This type of account still requires you to make a cash deposit, and federal law requires that you deposit at least $2,000 to open a margin account. However, you can borrow money and shares using a margin account. Typically, you can use 2:1 leverage. For example, if you have $5,000 in your margin account, you can purchase $10,000 worth of stock. Each account will have its own buying power, which is the amount you can fund. That is buying power is the amount of cash you have plus the amount you can borrow.

Company List

There are a large number of available brokers, and the best thing for you to do is go online and search for one to your liking. That said, here is a partial listing of brokerages:

- Ally Invest
- Charles Schwab
- E-Trade
- Fidelity Investments
- Interactive brokers
- Merrill Edge
- Robinhood
- Tasty Works/Tasty Trade
- TD Ameritrade
- Trade Station
- Vanguard

The best brokers for beginners include E-Trade, Robinhood, and TD Ameritrade. Each has its advantages and disadvantages. You will want to consider features available for analysis as well as commissions. Robinhood is a zero-commission broker.

Types of Orders

It's important for beginners to understand the different types of orders that they can place. People think that you can just buy and sell shares, but it's a little more involved than that.

The first type of order you can place is called a market order. This is what most people think about when considering buying and selling the stock. It's simply placing an order where you will buy or sell at the prevailing market price at that moment in time. You are telling the broker that you will accept whatever price they come up with, but it's going to be at or near the market price or "mark" that you see when you place the order in most cases.

Something you will want to look at when placing your orders is *bid* and *ask*. A bid is an amount that traders who want to buy a given stock are offering. Ask is the asking price sellers currently want. These figures change by the moment, but if there is a large bid-ask spread, it might take longer to find a buyer.

A limit order, in contrast, is an order that specifies a price that you are willing to accept when selling or a price you're willing to pay if you want to buy shares. If you are looking to get out of a stock quickly, a limit order can help you do that, since instead of selling at the market price you could sell at the bid price, which would mean a quick sale. Alternatively, you can use a limit order to hold out for a price that you are willing to accept even if you have to wait. A limit order could be placed as a buy order to only buy shares if the priced dropped to a certain level, or alternatively while selling you could decide only to sell when the price reached a certain point. Traders use limit orders in order to set pre-determined profit levels. You can create a limit order that expires at the end of the trading day, or use a good until canceled order that will sit out there until it's executed. It will be executed when a bid or ask matches your price.

A stop loss order is a type of limit order that is used to sell your shares automatically if the price drops to a certain level. Traders use this to protect themselves from large losses. As a long-term investor, you are probably not interested in stop-loss orders, because a long-term investor should keep their shares through downturns as well as rising stock markets if the shares help them meet their long-term goals.

GOAL * PLAN * SUCCESS

Chapter 10 Analysis and Herd Behavior

Before we get into the details of charting and technical analysis, we are going to describe what it's all about in general terms. It basically involves crowd behavior. One of the most famous sayings among traders is "the trend is your friend". That means the goal is to simply do what other people are doing – to a point.

Supply and Demand

Over the short-term, changes in stock prices are due to changes in supply and demand. When there are more people interested in buying a stock, sellers can hold out for higher prices. The prices that traders are willing to pay for a stock that is seen as more valuable can rise rapidly. On the other hand, when sellers are trying to get out quickly, they have to lower their asking prices. If a stock is seen in a negative light, people aren't willing to pay as much money in order to own it. In short, the basic rules of economics apply to stock prices.

Bid and Ask

This is reflected in two metrics used in pricing stocks, *bid* and *ask*. The current stock price that you see quoted on the market is called the market price, or mark. However, that doesn't mean you can buy or sell your shares for that price by the time you place your order. The bid for a given stock is the price that bidders are willing to pay for the stock. Ask is the price that sellers are asking for it. In order for a share of stock to sell, the bid and ask must come together. The difference in the bid and ask at any given moment is called the *bid-ask spread*.

In modern markets, things are happening at a quick pace. In most circumstances when you place a buy or sell order at the market price, you'll find another trader willing to accept your terms relatively quickly. On the other hand, if a stock is rapidly increasing or decreasing in value, it might be difficult to close a transaction. Prices can move fast, and by the time you place your order the price you need to move to in order to close the deal may have moved. If you need to sell a stock quick and the price is rapidly dropping, consider placing your trade as a limit order using the current bid price as your limit price. This will ensure a quick sale.

The role of emotion on the market

When money is involved, especially the prospect of losing or gaining a lot of money, emotions can become overwhelming. Fear and panic can set in when asset prices decline, leading people to sell off in large numbers. This deepens and speeds up the rate of decline. When prices are rising, people often become irrationally exuberant. With increasing enthusiasm and the appearance of greed, people

Chapter 11 Charts, Trends, and Ranging

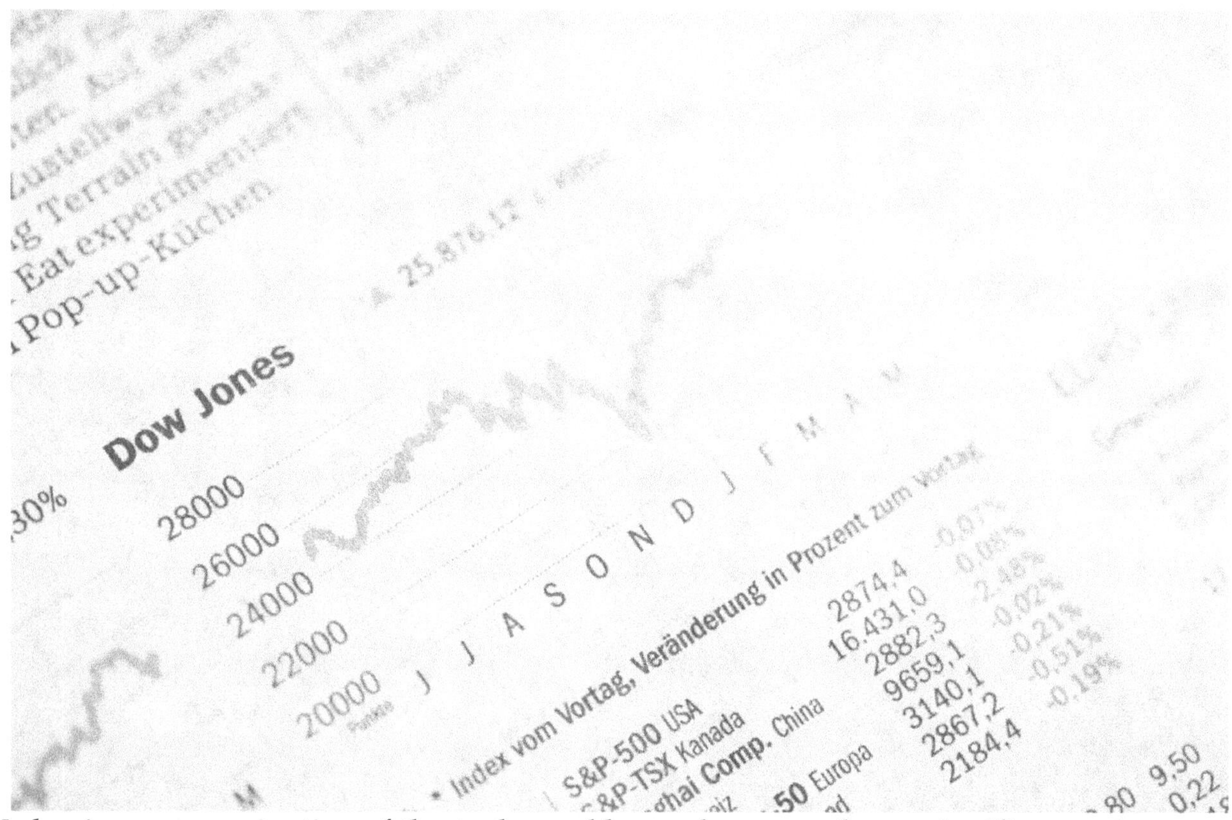

We begin our examination of the tools used by traders to seek out significant price movements by looking at trend analysis and ranging. The techniques described in this chapter are better described as *craft* rather than technical analysis, but they form the foundation of all that follows. Moreover, all traders use them from time to time. In short, you need to be able to eyeball charts to spot trends and pricing levels, and then use them to project ahead to determine future price points. Spotting trends is often the first step in analysis, with deeper examination using more sophisticated tools to confirm or reject the trend.

Trend lines

As a starting point, we use the simplest type of analysis you can do. That is, simply draw trend lines on your charts. In practice, you shouldn't rely on this alone, but it's a simple method that can be used in order to determine where a stock price *might* end up in the future. Other indicators will have to be used to confirm the appearance that a trend is in the making or will continue.

The procedure used to draw trend lines relies on the wavy shape of stock prices when they are graphed on a chart – that is they go up and down like an oscillator. There are three rules for trend lines:

- Look for an up and down swing in price that is moving in one direction or the other. It needs to revert or move back in the opposite direction to the main trend at least twice. If there are more of these points the trend line will be more accurate, but you have to use what you have.

- If the price is increasing, use the low points to anchor your trend line. Simply draw a straight line through each of the low points. Projecting out to the future will give you an estimate of where prices are going to end up.

- If the price is decreasing, draw your line through the peaks in the graph as the price declines. This will give you an estimate to the future, lower price of the stock.

In the example below, we have used an uptrend in a stock price to show you how to draw a trend line. Notice that had we drawn the line at an earlier time when we only had the two low points in the price oscillation, the end point of the line would have been fairly accurate in meeting the future price.

In the example below, we use the technique on a downward trend. Notice that the line is drawn through the peaks in the graph.

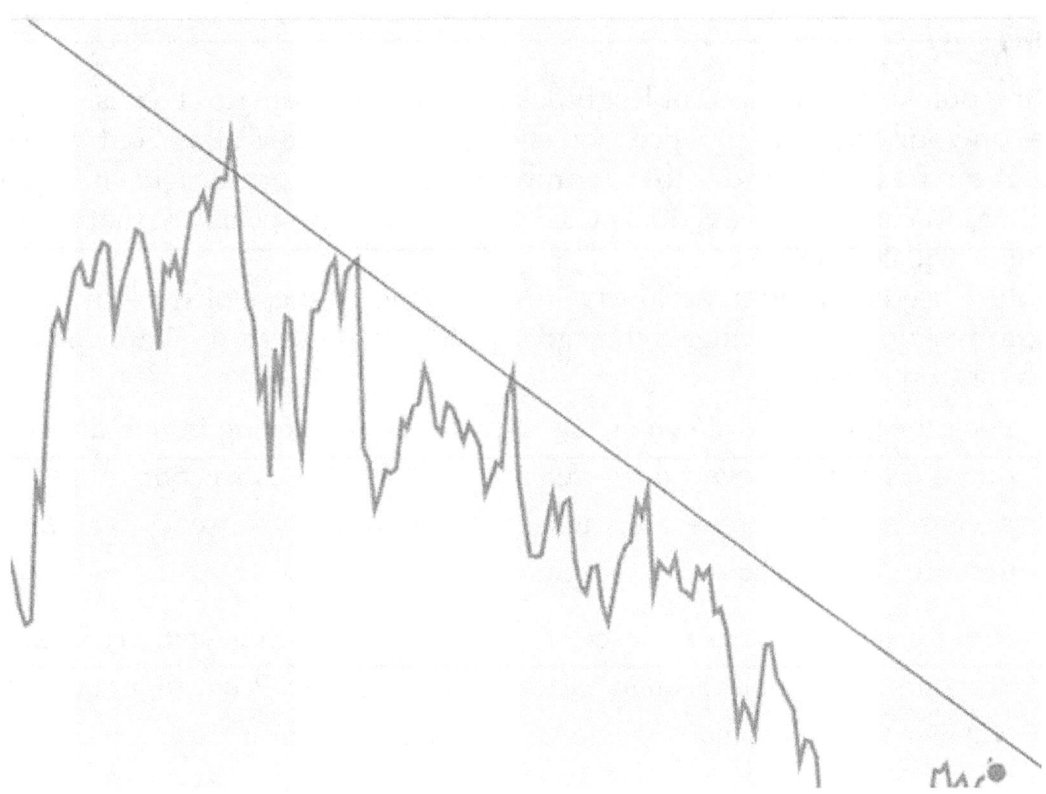

While trend lines can often be fairly accurate, they should only be used as a guideline in your decision making. A trend point is nothing more than eyeballing the chart. Many traders swear by trend lines, and those who master them can actually utilize them to enter into many successful trades. However the best approach is to use a trend line as a starting point for further analysis. Most stock charts that are available online allow you to draw lines directly on the charts.

Trading with the Trend

The simplest trading strategy is to simply follow the trend, and follow it for as long as you can. Once you've used a trend line to estimate where the stock price can go if it continues following the trend, you enter your position. Then place a limit order to sell your shares when the price reaches the point that you've determined the stock is going to reach if it continues rising.

Alternatively, you can short the stock when it's bearish. This is a technique that will be available for more advanced traders with margin accounts. In order to short the stock, you'll borrow the shares from the broker and sell them at the current market price. Of course you will need to keep close tabs on this kind of move – it could work against you.

After selling the shares, you wait for the stock price to drop to the level that you are expecting. Then you buy the shares on the market at the lower price. The difference in prices paid for the shares is your profit. You simply return the shares to the broker at that point.

You could simply trade with trends, and win some trades and lose some. But you can improve your odds by learning the tools of technical analysis to use in conjunction with your trend analysis.

Support

The next concept you need to be aware of is *support*. This is a pricing level that sets a lower boundary for the stock over a short time period. It's a low price that the stock won't drop beneath. So bulls and bears are balanced at this pricing level. Keep in mind that while zones of support can be useful to spot, that you'll need to look at other metrics to determine where price is going. In many cases, the stock price will keep touching the support pricing level and it simply won't drop below. It will bounce off the support price and go higher. However, that doesn't mean that at some point in the future the support level won't be breached. Candlesticks that will help you decide whether or not a breach is coming, or whether the stock is going to break to the upside instead. Moving averages can also help analyze these situations.

To find a level of support, draw a line through the lows of the stock price over a given time period. The level of support is taken to be the low price for the stock, for the present analysis.

In the chart below, we've drawn a line of support, shown as the horizontal line.

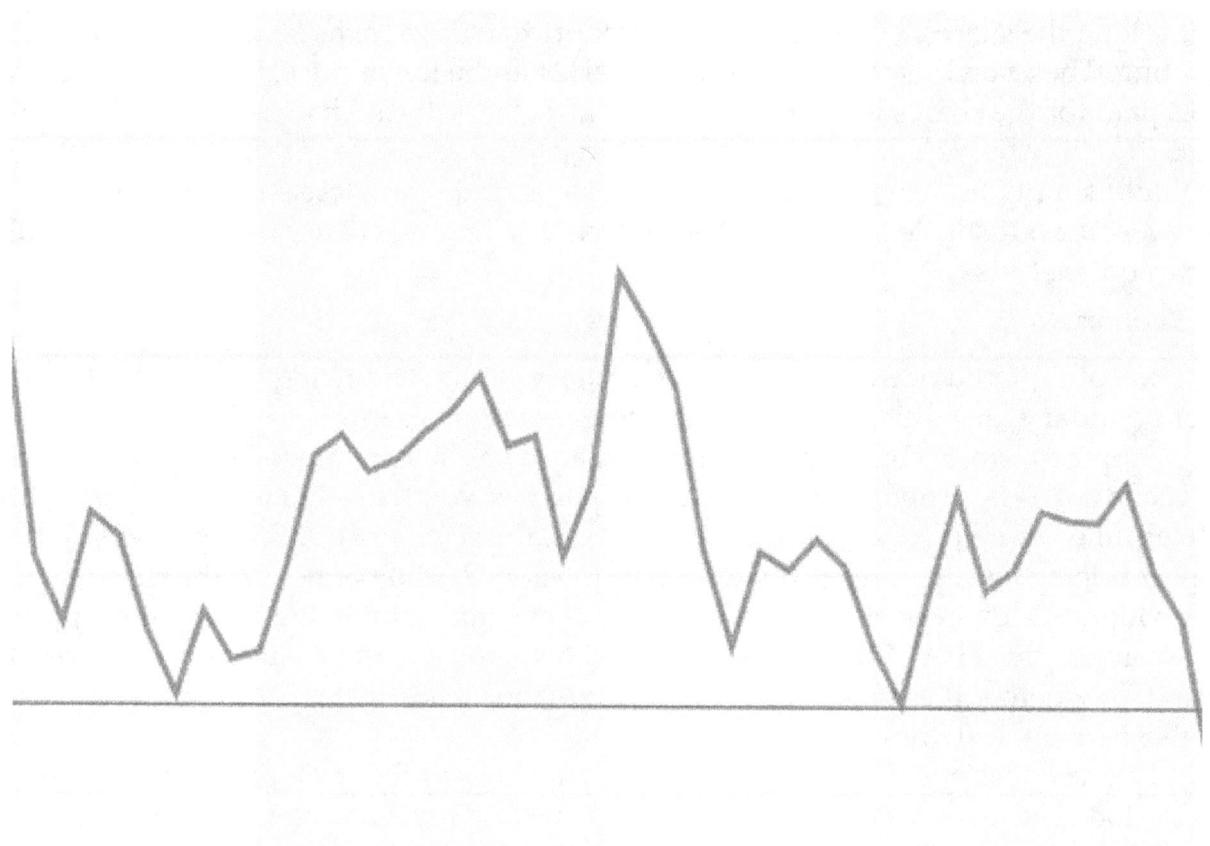

Notice that the stock touched the line twice. At a minimum, when deciding where a level of support is located, you must be able to see the stock price touch the line at least two times. It's better if it touches it more frequently. On the far right of the chart the price went slightly below the support line, but quickly returned to the support level. Remember that stock market data is incredibly noisy, so you'll have to look at data like that and ask yourself if the drip was statistically significant or not. To be a breach, it's got to be significant. Of course there will be other tools you can use to estimate the next move of the stock.

Resistance

Resistance is the flip-side of support. This is an upper boundary in pricing that the stock price can't cross. Bulls are able to bid up the price to the resistance level, but there isn't enough bullish sentiment to push prices higher. Resistance involves drawing a line through the peaks of the curve over a given time period. Again, the peaks of the price must touch the line at a minimum of two times.

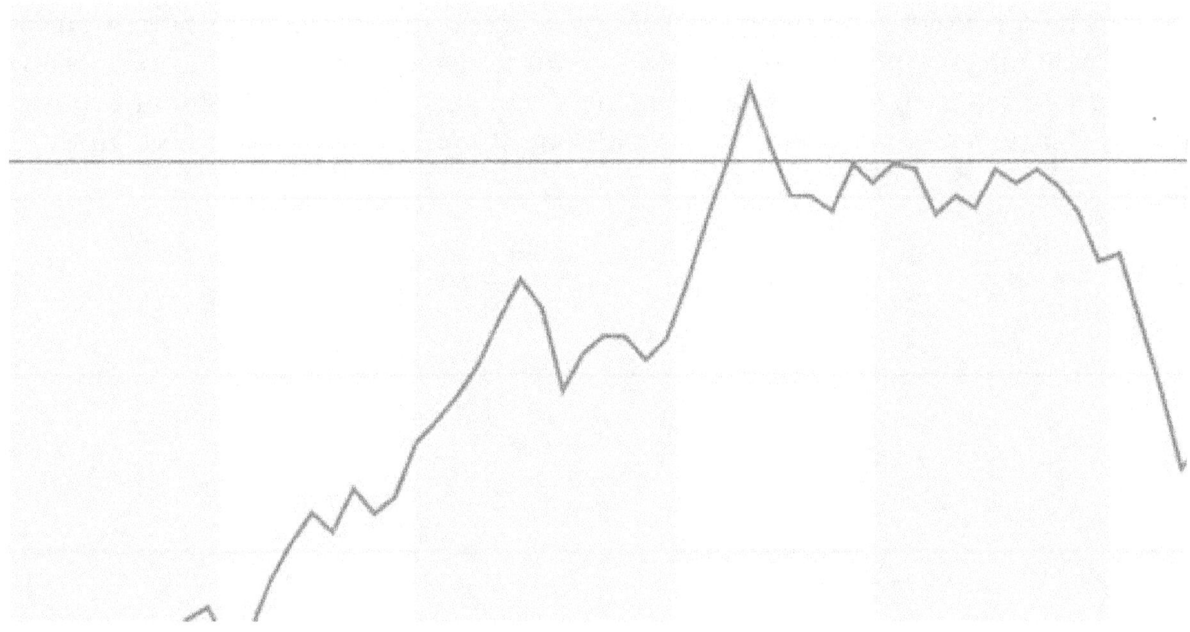

How to use support and resistance

Support is used to determine the low price of a stock over a given time period. Then, this can be used in different ways depending on how you are trading. First let's assume you are "long", so hoping to buy the shares in anticipation of a price increase. In that case, after you have determined the level of support, you wait until the stock price returns back to that price level. When it does, you enter your position. Then you'll wait for the stock to rise.

Support level can also be used to set a stop-loss order, to protect yourself if your estimate was wrong. The stop-loss can be set slightly below the support level. Remember because of random behavior the price might dip a little bit below the support level without really indicating that further drops in price are about to occur. To take an example, suppose that we determine the level of support is $50 a share. You could set your stop loss order at $49 a share. This means that if the stock dips to that price, our shares will be sold automatically. If the stock dipped to the downside then the stop-loss order will protect us from large losses.

Assuming that for our trade the stock stays in the trading range over a time period of interest, then we set a limit order to sell the shares a little bit below the resistance level. That means setting a level of profit when we enter the trade. Remember, you don't want to get greedy, and your entire life doesn't ride on the results of a single trade.

So the goal here is to set a decent level of profit on *this* trade. You don't let emotion come in and get you upset if the price happens to continue rising. You book your profits and then move forward to the next trade. A business that gets sustainable, regular profits is the one that survives. You want to keep that thought in mind as you proceed with your trades.

Ranges

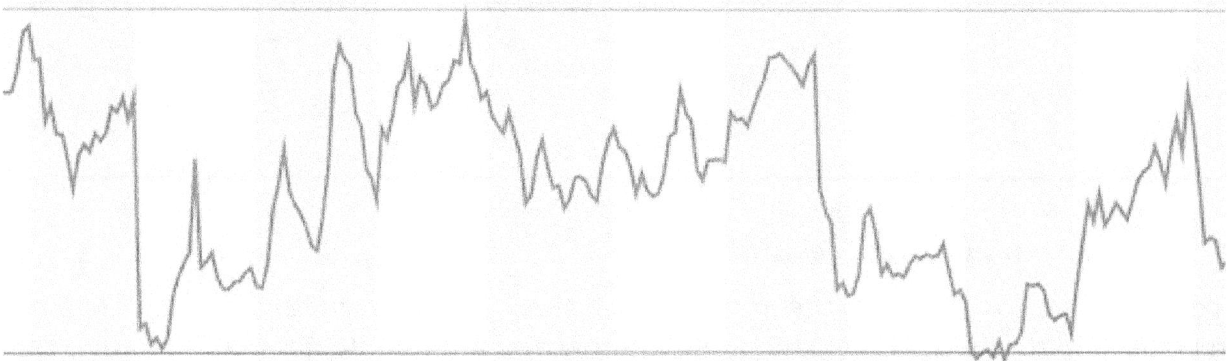

Sometimes a stock will repeatedly swing between two pricing levels for a relatively extended period of time. That is, it is trading within a range. The range can be estimated by drawing levels of support and resistance on the same chart.

In the above chart, the price level of resistance is indicated by the upper red line. The price level for support is indicated by the lower, purple line. Ranges can last for any length of time, and can even go on for months. The key to finding a trading range is that it lasts over a time frame that is of interest in your particular case. Remember that trade ranges don't last forever, at some point there will be a breakout to the upside or the downside, and the stock will settle in with a new level of support and/or resistance. These are guidelines only.

Trading Strategy for Ranges

However, notice that the price fluctuations within the range offer opportunities for profit.

It's possible that you will miss out on the upside, but a smart trader takes a methodical approach. Rather than being greedy or waiting around to see if the price might continue increasing, the smart trader sets up rules for their trade beforehand, and they stick to their rules. It's better to ensure a limited profit and duplicate the process, than it is to wait too long hoping for higher highs and find yourself losing money. Unfortunately that happens all too often.

Chapter 12 Fundamental Analysis

When it comes to determining which stocks, and therefore which companies, are going to be the most likely to continue to produce dividends in the long run, one of the best ways to go about doing so is through the process of fundamental analysis. Fundamental analysis works on the economy as a whole or on specific industries, depending on where you want to start.

Fundamental analysis answers a host of differing questions including:

- Is the company being straightforward about its profits?

- Is it able to reliably pay its debts?

- Is it currently turning a profit?

- Is it strong enough to continue being profitable in the long-term?

- Is its revenue moving in the right direction?

While these can be extremely involved questions, they all essentially boil down to the decision of whether or not a company is a good investment and if they are likely to continue producing dividends in the long-term. Fundamental analysis can also be thought of as a type of toolbox that can make answering this question much easier.

Quantitative and Qualitative analysis

Fundamental analysis is all about researching the fundamentals of a given company, but that alone won't be enough to tell you what you need to know unless you know what fundamentals you are working with to start. Unfortunately, this can be more comprehensive than you might hope as the fundamentals can include practically anything that affects the economic viability of your chosen company in one way or another. Basic fundamentals include things such as profit or revenue.

Generally speaking, different fundamental factors can be classified in two ways, quantitative and qualitative. Quantitative factors are those that are purely numerical in nature, things that will be written down and discussed during the next investors' meeting. Qualitative factors are those that focus more on the inherent qualities of the company and the things that make it great, which naturally makes them more difficult to track. Qualitative factors are generally less tangible and include things like its name recognition, the patents it holds and the quality of its board members.

Neither of these two types of factors is inherently superior to one another and they actually provide the greatest results when they are used in conjunction with one another. For example, consider the Coca-Cola Company. For quantitative factors, an analyst could look at its P/E ratio, earnings per share and, of course, its annual dividend payout rate. For qualitative factors, you would need to consider its overall brand recognition which takes it from a company that essentially sells carbonated sugar water to a company that is recognized by almost everyone on the planet. While this figure can't be quantified with a dollar amount it is, without a doubt, one of the major contributing factors to its overall success.

Assumptions

Intrinsic value is the true value of a company, regardless of what its stock price might be at the moment. One of the most important assumptions when it comes to fundamental analysis is that the stock market doesn't always reflect the real value of a particular company which is why fundamental analysis is needed in the first place. As an example, let's say you come across a stock that is currently worth $20 but, after doing your homework you establish that it has a real value of $25 instead. As the intrinsic value is greater than the current stock value then you know that this is a stock worth watching. Another crucial assumption is that the stock market will eventually reflect the intrinsic value of a company when given enough time. This realignment might happen in days, or it might take years, the only certainty is that it will happen eventually. This is at the heart of why fundamental analysis is so useful as by focusing on a particular company you will be able to suss out its intrinsic value and then find opportunities where the market has not kept up, buying into companies and receiving dividends that are only going to increase as the price of the company catches up to its true value.

There are two primary unknowns when it comes to fundamental analysis:

- It is difficult to determine if an estimated intrinsic value is correct due to the qualitative factors;

- It is difficult to determine how long it will take for the market to catch up to its intrinsic value.

Important qualitative factors to consider

Business model

The first thing that you are going to want to do when you catch wind of a company that might be worth following up on is to check out its business model which is more or less a generalization of how it makes its money. You can typically find these sorts of details on the company website or in its 10-K filing.

While this can be pretty straightforward, such as the Coca-Cola Company's business model of selling carbonated sugar water to the masses, sometimes it can be more complicated than you initially anticipated which is why it is always a good idea to do your homework before making any assumptions. A good example of why this is the case can be seen in Boston Chicken Inc. which was a popular company in the early 90s. You see, despite the name, Boston Chicken Inc. didn't actually make a profit selling chicken. Instead, it sold extremely overpriced franchises to individuals and then made money on loans with exceedingly high interest and royalty fees from individuals using their name. When news of how they actually made their money got out, the company went from darling of Wall Street to delisted in a matter of months.

When it comes to choosing companies to invest in, it is also important that you understand the business model of the companies you invest in. This will make it easier for you to ensure that your investments are going to continue moving in a positive direction in the long run. It will make it possible for you to understand its drivers when it comes to future growth and help to protect you from being blindsided by unexpected developments.

Competitive advantage

It is also important to consider the various competitive advantages that the company you have your eye on might have over its competition. Companies that are going to be successful in the long-term are always going to have an advantage over their competition in one of two ways. They can either have better operational effectiveness or improved strategic positioning. Operational effectiveness is the name given to doing the same things as the competition but in a more efficient and effective way. Strategic positioning occurs when a company gains an edge by doing things that nobody else is doing. Competitive advantage comes in two types, operational effectiveness, and strategic positioning. Operational effectiveness occurs when a company is simply better at doing the things that it and its competitors do. Strategic positioning occurs when a company gets a leg up on its competition by out maneuvering its rivals by finding the same end result through different means or simply doing things its competition isn't doing. In general, a company can't maintain a competitive advantage by doing the same things just as well as its competition. There are a few different ways to generate competitive advantage, including:

- Maintaining a reliable amount of operational effectiveness

- Maintaining a strong activity system that promotes sustainability

- Continuing to perform activities that are uniquely tailored to the strategy of the company.

- Offering clear choices to its customers when compared to its competition

- Creating a unique competitive position

Leadership

The type of management that is currently leading a company is going to go a long way towards determining if it is going to be successful in the long run. After all, even the most well thought out business plan will fail without being able to rely on the right infrastructure to support it in the long run. When it comes to analyzing management, the first place you are going to want to look is the corporate information section of the company's website. This won't provide you with much more than the names of the folks at the top, but if they have been around the block then names should be enough to pull up everything you need to know about their past work experiences. While this might not ultimately amount to much if there is something unfortunate in their past this should bring it to light.

Market Overview

The best time to use fundamental analysis is when you are looking to gain a broad idea of the state of the market as it stands and how that relates to the state of things in the near future when it comes time to actually trading successfully. Regardless of what market you are considering, the end goals are the same, find the most effective trade for the time period that you are targeting.

Find a baseline

When it comes to looking at the current state of the fundamentals, the first thing that you are going to want to do is come up with a baseline for the underlying asset related to the potential trade in question, otherwise you will have no reliable way of knowing what the current state of the trade actually means. For the best results, you will then want this analysis to factor in data from both the macro and the micro levels as you will need both to accurately gather all the data you will be looking for. Remember, no market operates in a vacuum and if you find the small linchpins of data on which the major moves turn then you will know where to be in order to take the fullest advantage of it possible. Fundamental analysis hinges on the belief that past market movement is a reliable indicator of future movement which means it will tell you where the next big thing is likely to hit before it does.

It doesn't matter what market you are working with; all underlying assets go through numerous different phases depending on how popular they are in the moment. If the asset is currently in a period of extreme popularity, then you will find that volatility is down while liquidity is up. Once this period can no longer be sustained the asset enters what is known as the bust period where you will notice a decrease in liquidity and an increase in volatility. There are also sub categories based on how recently the asset entered the phase in question.

Decide on the phase of the market

This step is relatively straightforward as if the market as a whole is in a boom state then liquidity will be high across the board and volatility will be low, likewise if things are currently in a bust state then volatility will be high and liquidity will be low in all corners. It is important to utilize the proper quantitative techniques when doing so that you draw your own conclusions instead of listening to what pundits or paid analysts think on the matter. While going with what the pros say will work occasionally, finding your own undervalued currency pairs will allow you to get in on the best trades ahead of the pack.

Consider emerging trends

Once you have a clear idea of what type of phase the market as a whole is in, the next thing you are going to want to determine relevant areas that are likely going to be the cause of the next round of changes that the global market goes through. These types of movements are likely to come from major economic powers with those at the top of the list being obvious choices for further study. In a boom period, there are likely to be numerous emerging trends which can make it difficult to back the right horse. This is not a problem when it comes to a bust market, however, as the emerging trends are likely going to be fewer in number as well as farther between overall.

Decide what is likely to experience the most growth in this part of the cycle

Once you have a clear idea of the current state of things, the next thing you will want to focus on are sectors that you feel are going to experience major growth as the current boom or bust phase plays itself out. This could be things like new technology, new market fundamentals or new political leanings as well as a host of similar scenarios; regardless, finding scenarios that lead to an increase in productivity is a great way to home in on the markets that you can ensure are on the qualitative target.

Put it all together

Once you have a clear idea of what the market should look like as well as what may be on the horizon, the next step is to put it all together to compare what has been and what might to what the current state of the market is. Not only will this give you a realistic idea of what other investors are going to do if certain events occur the way they have in the past, you will also be able to use these details in order to identify underlying assets that are currently on the cusp of generating the type of movement that you need if you want to utilize them in the future.

The best time to get on board with a new underlying asset is when it is nearing the end of the post-bust period or the end of a post-boom period depending on if you are going to place a call or a put. In these scenarios, you are going to have the greatest access to the freedom of the market and thus have access to the greatest overall allowable risk that you are going to find in any market. Remember, the amount of risk that you can successfully handle without an increase in the likelihood of failure is going to start decreasing as soon as the boom or bust phase begins in earnest so it is important to get in as quickly as possible if you hope to truly maximize your profits.

Understand the relative strength of any given trade

When an underlying asset is experiencing a boom phase, the strength of its related fundamentals is going to be what determines the way that other investors are going to act when it comes to binary options trading. Keeping this in mind it then stands to reason that the earlier a given underlying asset is in a particular boom phase, the stronger the market surrounding it is going to be. Remember, when it comes to fundamental analysis what an underlying asset looks like at the moment isn't nearly as important as what it is likely to look like in the future and the best way to determine those details is by keeping an eye on the past.

Chapter 13 Technical Analysis

Know your charts

Price charts

A price chart is a core part of technical analysis; essentially, it is a chart with both an x and a y axis where the price can be seen along the vertical axis and the time can be seen along the horizontal axis. While there are plenty of different charts to choose from, each with their own unique strengths and weaknesses, those that you will want to keep in mind early on include the line chart, the candlestick chart, the bar chart, and the point and click chart.

Line chart

The line chart is the simplest of all the charts because all it does is showing the closing price of a given stock over a set period of time. The lines, in this case, are formed once the grouping of closing prices has been determined and then connected with the end goal of showing a trend. You won't be able to find details such as what the opening price for the same period of time was or what the overall results for the day were but you will be able to determine if the day over day is positive, which is still quite important, which is why this is one of the first charts that day traders of all skill levels consult when they are looking into the details of a new stock.

Example of line chart: Apple Inc. (ticker: AAPL, July 2002 - May 2019)

Candlestick chart

Another worthwhile technical analysis tool that you are going to want to be familiar with is the candlestick. They provide important data for traders across multiple time frames by creating what is known as price bars. Each day will provide you with details regarding the high, open, close and low points of the stock each day. These details can be used to build patterns that make it easier to predict how the price is likely going to move in the future.

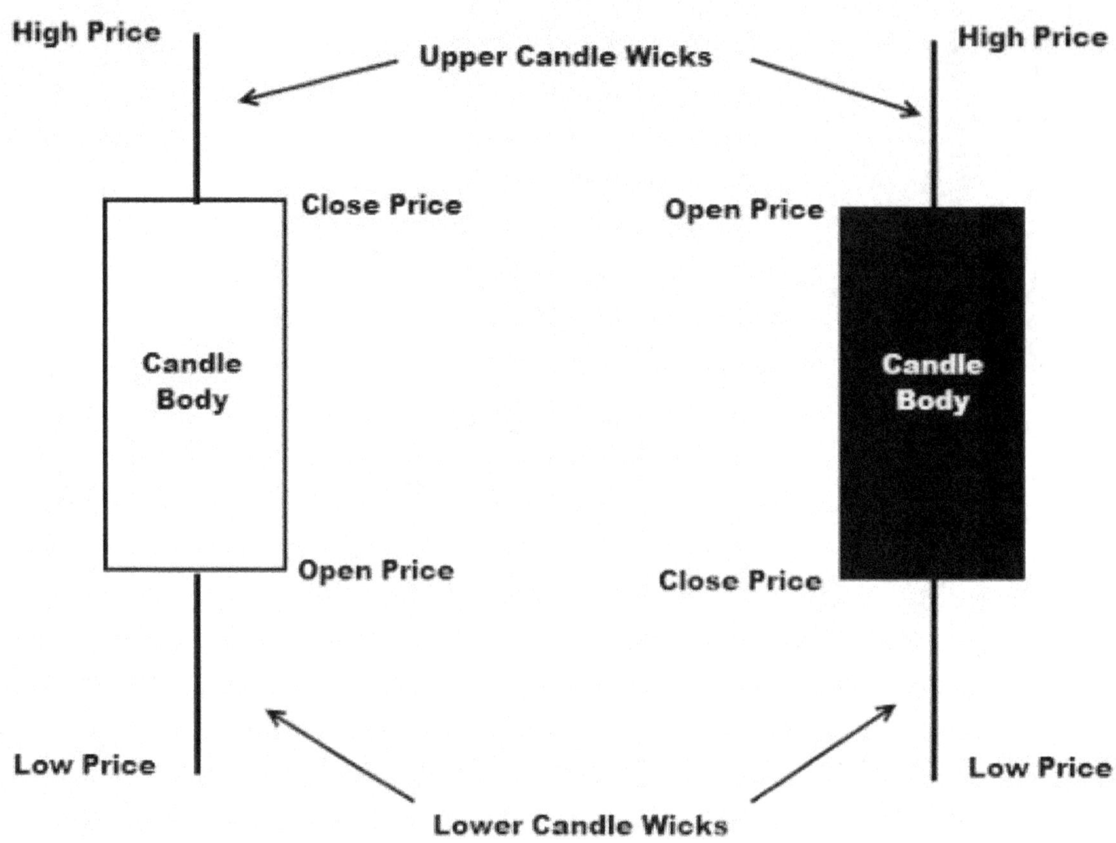

The candlesticks that are going to be the most accurate when it comes to plotting the price of stocks are going to fall into two types, continuations, and reversals. Reversal candlestick patterns tend to predict a coming change in the current pricing trends. Meanwhile, continuation patterns predict that the current price action is simply going to continue as is.

A candlestick chart is similar to a bar chart, though the information it provides is much more detailed overall. Like a bar chart, it includes a line to indicate the range for the day, however, when you are looking at a candlestick chart you will notice a wide bar near the vertical line which indicates the degree of difference the price saw throughout the day. If the price that the stock is trading at increases overall for the day, then the candlestick will often be clear while if the price has decreased then the candlestick is going to be red.

Example of candlestick chart: McDonald's Corporation (ticker: MCD)

Point and figure chart

While the point and figure chart aren't used as much as it once was, it has been in use for more than 100 years which means there is still plenty of use left in it. The point and figure chart is useful when you want to know the movement of prices, without worrying about volume or time spent. This makes it a pure pricing indicator without much of the noise that many other charts need to deal with. It is also useful if the other types of charts contain information that is skewing them in one way or the other.

When you first see a point and figure chart you will always be able to tell because it is comprised of lines of Xs and Os instead of points and lines. In this instance, the Xs are going to indicate periods of positive trends while Os will represent downward trends. The numbers and letters along the bottom of the chart indicate months and date estimates. Point and click charts also include a set of reversal criteria that is set by the trader looking at the chart, these criteria consider the amount the price is going to move in order for an X to become an O or vice a versa. As the trend changes, it shifts right to indicate this fact.

Example of pint-and-figure chart: McDonald's Corporation (ticker: MCD)

Support and resistance

Understanding support and resistance is crucial to achieving the success you are looking for when it comes to technical analysis and while they may seem complex at first, they will become clearer every time you put the theory around them into practice. At their most basic, resistance can be thought of as the ceiling on the price of a particular currency or currency pair which means the price is unlikely to move past this point while support can be thought of as the price floor where it is unlikely to decrease any further.

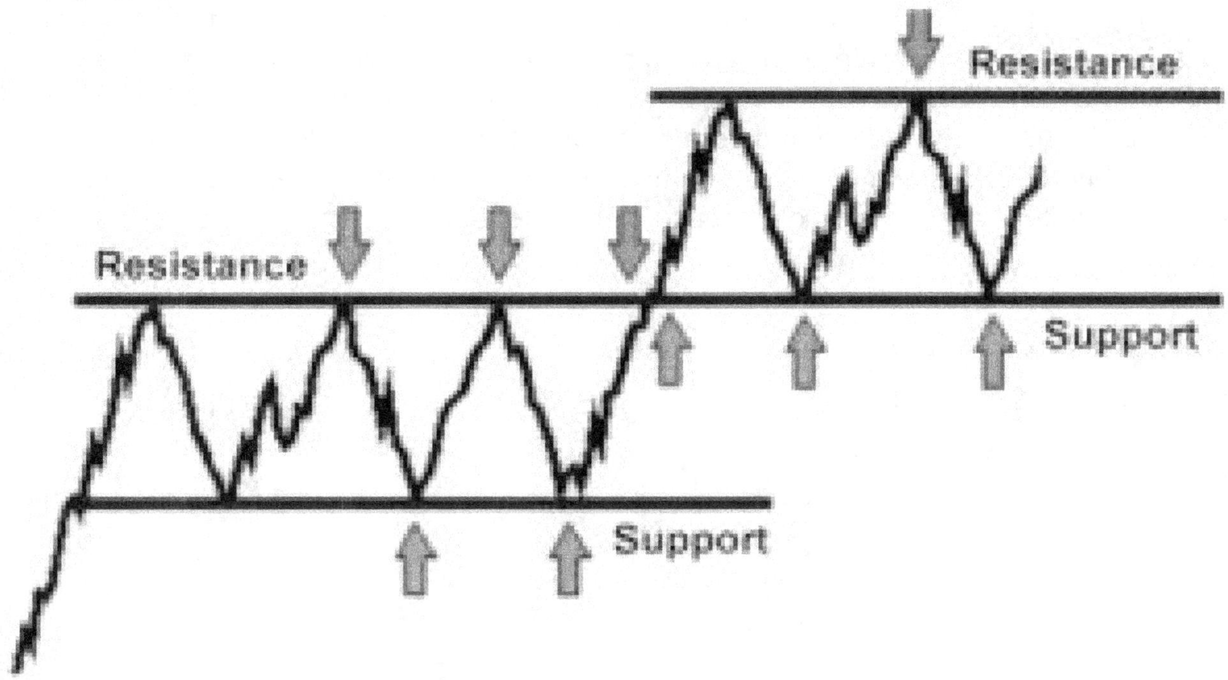

Trend lines

While it is not uncommon for these ceilings and floors to change on a regular basis, being prepared for these changes is what separates the novice traders from the experts. Understanding these movements is done through the use of trend lines. When the market is trending upward then new resistance levels are going to be formed as that upward price movement begins to slow before starting its trek back down the trendline. This is likely to happen when uncertainty rises in regards to a given stock. This will, in turn, creates what is known as a short-term top which is essentially a temporary price plateau in the overall movement pattern.

Shorter trends can actually be part of trends that are much longer overall, which is why it is important to always double check and ensure you aren't making a move on something that is only an offshoot of a much larger, and much different trend. To make the process of deciding what's what even easier, it is important to always keep an eye on the weekly, daily and yearly charts if you want to locate any truly long-term trends. If you are looking to get rich quick, however, then you will want to stick to the daily charts instead.

After you have found an especially interesting trend, the next step is going to be drawing a trendline which is as simple as drawing a straight line that correctly illustrates the direction the trend is currently moving in. When it comes to an uptrend, you will want to draw your line in such a way that it connects the dots of all of the lows in such a way that the line is below the relevant data. If you are looking at a reversal trend then you are going to want to draw the line so that it connects the highs, leaving the data below the trendline.

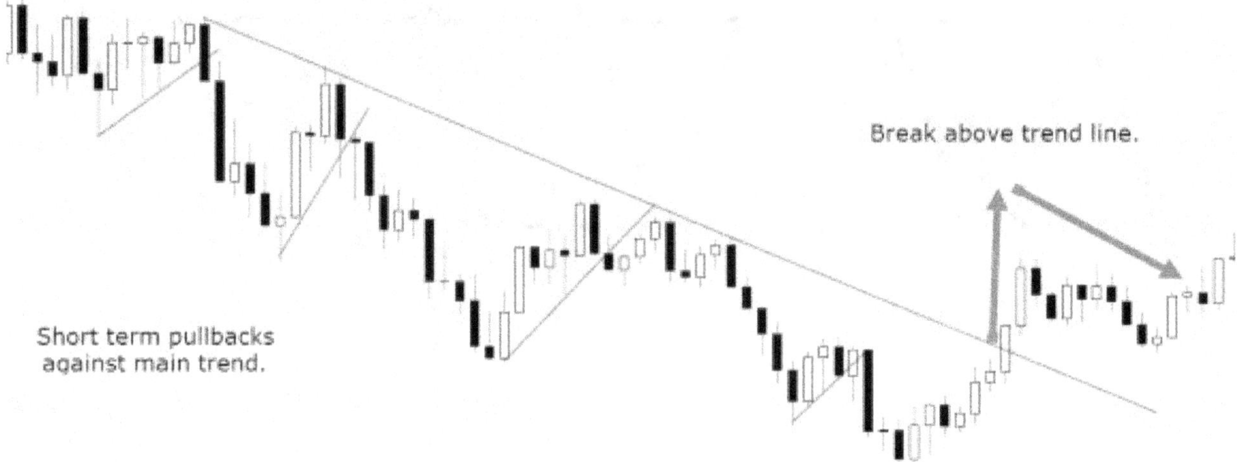

It is important to start paying extremely close attention to the price of the stock that you are watching when it begins to again reach the point where the trendline begins to broaden as this is likely to be the point where the price is going to cease its downward fall. It is important to note in instances such as this that a trendline can lend support to a given stock for a significant period of time while changing very little in the interim. Likewise, if the market is in a downward trend overall then you will want to be on the lookout for a set of peaks at a declining angle and a trendline that connects the point of each peak together. As the price gets closer to the trendline you are going to want to be on the lookout for indicators that point towards selling as this is how the price was likely pushed lower previously as well.

You will also want to keep an eye out for channel lines which are a pair of lines to the side of the data you are watching that indicate the levels of resistance and support that are in play. One trendline connects the highs while the other connects the lows while the resulting channel can either go up or down, or even sideways, but the interpretation will always remain constant. The goal should be to establish a channel that is long enough to show a break from the data that it has been following. This breakout point will mark the best time to get in on the trend you are following to ensure that you have the maximum amount of time to profit from the trend you have discovered.

Range

Trading based on range is the opposite of trading based on trend in several important ways. The first of these is that it offers up a much smaller overall level of risk, though the potential for gain is likewise mitigated as well. The range makes no special distinction when it comes to the direction an underlying asset moves because the logic behind range trading states that the price of the asset is always likely to return to at or near the point it originally started at. As such, it is common for range traders to actually bet on the fact that prices will move the same levels numerous times which means the skilled trader can trade these same levels time and again.

Another key fact about trading based on the range is that it is not as important to find the best entry point possible as it is to find a situation where you can build towards a strong trading position. Unlike when trading based on trend it is better to stick with larger overall trades assuming you have the bankroll to hold out until profits begin to be generated.

Moving averages

In order to make identifying trends as easy as possible, you are going to want to pay attention to what are known as moving averages. A moving average is calculated based on the average price of a stock over a specific period of time. For example, the moving average of a given day can be calculated according to the price of the stock in question based on the average price it held for the past 20 days. Connecting all these points on the chart will form the moving average line for that stock.

Round price levels

Finally, when it comes to determining the current levels of support or resistance then you can be safe in assuming that the points where the price stagnates are typically going to be round numbers. What this means in a practical sense is that there will likely be several repeat positions at or around the numbers in question for both the level of resistance as well as the level of support. This, in turn, then means that you can be fairly certain that the price will not creep past these numbers.

Chapter 14 The 10 Guidelines for Right Trading Mindset

One of the most important things any trader can have is the right trading mindset. This refers to the ability to remain cool and collected every day of the week. Trading stocks is done successfully by those who understand the essence of remaining calm at any given situation in order to carefully monitor something within their proximity.

It is important to understand that enduring surprises time and again will increase your chances of incurring losses when stock trading. You must remain calm and collected, developing a trading mindset that eventually dictates different patterns of your life. For instance, you might have to start waking up late at night or in the early hours of the morning in order to follow up on investment. Also, you might have to choose entirely new reading material from your normal information sources, changing the nature and composition of information that you absorb.

Either way, learning to have a positive mindset is pivotal in ensuring that you can attain any kind of success when you start trading. It is necessary to point out that inspiration will always come from within yourself so never go looking for it too far.

Guideline 1: Utilize Technology

Most people underestimate the power of technology in the modern world when it comes to driving different fundamental aspects of life. Technology has been responsible for massive changes in terms of developments and spreading information. You should utilize every bit of technology available to you to somehow ease the process of trading. You should be able to acquire information on the stocks you are interested in with relative ease because of the technology access available to you. There are better methods of communication today than in the past, information moves much faster than in the past and it is possible to make the entire world into a small global online village through social media.

Therefore, there is no excuse not to search for software that and guide you on setting pivot points, stop-losses and even entry points. There are different types of technology that you can utilize in order to get you in the right trading mindset. This way, you can focus on other fundamental aspects of trading while still ensuring that profitability is a guarantee. It is amazing how simple technology works to put you just in the right frame of mind to handle specific challenges that face you as you trade.

Guideline 2: Always Use a Stop-loss

In case you are not familiar with the importance of a stop-loss, this prevents you from making losses when a trade starts making losses. It limits the loss cap for your money, ensuring that you exit a trade just as you hit the stop-loss level. This has the disadvantage of missing out in case the trade suddenly changes and witnesses the boom that you were anticipating. Either way, a stop loss will enable you to be in the right trading mindset because you will not always be fidgety about losing a large amount of money on a single trade.

It will be possible to save your funds for a future trade by relying on a stop-loss even if the trade was to change and start moving into a profitable position. Patience is key when trading and this is epitomized by a stop-loss. A trade that is unstable can easily make you massive losses, so being cautious about the value movements of the trade is critical for success. A stop loss is a necessary risk-tackling measure that you must make particularly if you have immediate short-term goals that must be achieved for the success of the trade.

Guideline 3: Become a Student

A quick way of becoming successful is becoming a student of the very markets you intend to trade-in. At first, make small and few trades, listening to advice and gauging the market with the knowledge that you already have. There is never a time to stop learning because even if you achieve short-term success, massive losses can easily await you in the near future. Do not underestimate the value of continuously learning because if you observe closely, you will realize that even the expert traders take some time out to learn for themselves.

There are various ways you can become a student; for instance, you can work under the apprenticeship of a master. This does not mean that they set up a trading account, you must show your own commitment by setting up an even trying a trade for yourself. Thereafter, ask a professional trader that you might know of to teach you the ropes of trading so that you can also profit. You can also identify stock market websites that specialize in providing news and other trading-related facts that will help you develop a trading routine and, eventually the right trading mindset.

Guideline 4: A Plan is Important

There is nothing more important than having the right trading plan because, without it, you can never be in the right trading mindset for success. A plan identifies your objectives and the methodology you will use when approaching different challenges. On the off chance that you want to identify your risks, then this makes an important element of the plan you intend to implement.

Remember that you must set everything you want to do in pen or paper or even on an Excel worksheet. Identify the main aspects of trade you want to implement and take into careful consideration the resources you have. One of the most significant parts of the trading plan is the element of time because you must plan for it in an appropriate manner. Remember that time is everything and once lost, it is impossible to recover. A proper plan will set you in the right mood for trading because you will be able to envision whatever you want to implement. You will have foreseen some problems and usually, this is enough to ensure success. Therefore, take some time and plan before launching into your first trade.

Guideline 5: Identify Rest Periods Beforehand

As much as it is important to constantly stay on the loop as you will soon discover when you start trading, having a rest is equally important. You might want to continuously trade and make money because of the ongoing opportunities right before you. However, what is more, important is investing in time for yourself as well as family and friends because it makes all the difference in having the right trading mindset. When you overwork yourself, you can be sure that you will never be in the right trading mindset. Have a conversation with the people close to you; understand what is going on in their lives. This is just as important to you as the trading process and you must always recognize those who are close and around you. Set limits for the time you trade and do not bog yourself down in front of a computer screen attempting to profit on a late trade; if it is time for bed, it is time for bed. You must recognize the importance of giving yourself a rest because you can only produce to your best when you are fresh and full of energy to go.

Guideline 6: Make Sure Trading is a Business to You

Avoid constantly taking money out of your account just to spend it on something simple and unnecessary when one of your trades has come right. Instead, plow the money back into the trade and identify your losses or profits. Try to use as much money as possible in order to spread different trades and minimize the risk of incurring losses. When you think of your trades just like a business and the thing to put food on your plate, then you are on the right track to achieving success.

Guideline 7: Make Sure Your Trading Practices are Reasonable

If you have $2,000 in your trading account, do not trade it all away; instead, look for minimalist strategies that will allow you to trade on multiple exchanges and try to profit. This way, you spread the risk through several trades and increase your income when a majority of them come right. You will not be pressured for all your trades to go right because only a few from your choices will be sufficient to cover your losses and produce a profit, as well.

Guideline 8: Planning for Trading Capital is Important

When you understand the importance of your trading capital, you are able to make trading a continuous practice and constantly profiting. Just as your trades need to be reasonable, ensure that you have a back-up for your trading capital for the same amount. These are some of the things that make trading quite difficult and must be considered in order to provoke some success. Your trading capital will always give you an advantage when you make losses because you will have gained crucial information on a specific market and able to turn to your substitute capital in order to make profits.

Guideline 9: Have a Trading Methodology

When you have a consistent method of trading, it empowers you to make the right decision in terms of your investments in the stocks. This certainly sets you in the right mindset because you can identify favorable spots in the market and utilize them appropriately. A right trading mindset is enhanced by an appropriate approach to trading that you have developed and is suitable for utilizing your strengths to guarantee success. A trading methodology sets you in the right frame of mind for trading because you will be able to view most of the challenges you encounter in a positive way.

Guideline 10: Do Not Risk Too Much

Most people end up risking much more than they really can afford to, and this leads to their demise. You have heard of stories where consistent traders who were once making a living from the stock market now completely out of cash and living in dire conditions. Most people usually use these stories as an example to keep from trading, but the truth is that you should only bite off what you can chew.

If you put your entire life savings in a trade without a back-up, it will be your fault if you lose all the money and have to start a new life. Never risk more than you need to because you should always trade within your limits to grow. It is the only sure way of achieving success because the benefits of trade will not come immediately, but to those who are patient enough to wait.

Conclusion

Stocks represent a unit of ownership in a company. Even though a stock does not give the stockholder the right to take possession of a company's assets, it gives them the right to vote and take part in the decision-making process. There exist two types of stocks: the preferred stock and common stock. The common stock is the one that gives the holder the rights to vote and have a part in the decision-making process during stockholder meetings, but they are also owners in the company, so their claim in the event of a dissolution or bankruptcy comes last. On the other hand, the preferred stock gives the holder the status of a lender, which means that they are paid first in the event of a dissolution or bankruptcy. Stocks are issued to help companies raise money through an intricate process known as the IPO. While the investment bank strategy of underwriting during initial public offerings is the more common of all issuance strategies, some companies choose to offer their shares directly to the public or leave the public to set their own prices through an auction. This initial price then forms the base price at which future trading will be conducted.

Bonds are issued by governments and corporate institutions that need to raise huge amounts of capital for massive expenditure. Investment is the most common motive behind bond issuance, but recurrent expenditures and debt restructuring is also a common motivation for a company or government issuing a bond. Unlike stocks, bonds mature at a set time, carry a specific interest or coupon yield, and are issued at fixed face value. The price fluctuations of bonds, while present, are very slight. They are usually caused by changing interest rates and demand close to maturity. There are two main types of bonds: *zero-coupon bonds*, which are issued at a discount to the yield, and *convertible bonds*, which allow holders to convert their bond capital into shareholding in a company. Callable bonds may be redeemed by the issuer at any time, which means that the investor could lose some good money when their investment is not allowed to mature or is called back at the point when interest rates are most favorable for great capital gains. The stock markets of the world started as a group of debt collectors organizing to renegotiate and exchange equity in ancient France. Over close to millennia, the stock market has spread to the rest of the world. Stock markets have also become more innovative, incorporating new technologies as they came up and growing through economic downturns, stock market crashes, and world wars. Currently, the world's stock markets are almost combined in one giant bourse, with mergers like the Euronext and NYSE in 2007 creating a transatlantic stock market. Other international stock markets include the NASDAQ OMX and Euronext itself, which combined the stock markets of Spain, Belgium, and the Netherlands. This linkage has not been without its fair share of complications. The stock market crashes of 1987 and 2008 affected large portions of the world bourses and shed off massive amounts of wealth from investors all around the world.

Finally, short-term investing represents a tail end part of long-term investing that is rather similar to trading. But for people with a short-term goal, such as care or house purchase, short-term investing requires you to combine the tenets of long-term investing and trading and become either an active short-term investor or an inert one.